Anti-Sell

Marketing, Lead Generation & Networking Tips for Freelancers Who Hate Sales

Steve Morgan

Contents

Introduction

"Repeat after me: I. Hate. Sales."

I hate sales. Honestly, I really do. I've been freelancing full-time for over five years now, and even so, I still hate sales. I hate it as much now as I did when I first started out. It's the process and the idea that people have to pay me money for doing the work that I love. I just want to do my 'work' – not do sales. But at the same time, you may not be happy working for an employer, preferring to do the work in your own name and in your own right instead.

If you've picked up this book then I'm guessing that you're either considering becoming a freelancer or are one already. First things first: congratulations! You've made (or are making) a hell of a good decision – take that from me.

Freelancing is great because you get to be in control of everything – the type of work you do, the amount of work you do, how to structure the work, how/where/when you do it, and so on. Absolutely everything.

Conversely, the only problem is that it's *you* who is in control of everything, which includes everything to do with running a business that you mightn't have thought you'd be signing up to when you came up with your business idea. To explain, this other side of the coin covers things that if you were still an employee working in someone else's business, it would be taken care of by somebody else. These include admin, finance, and – of course – sales.

A great bit of self-employment advice is that you should do what you enjoy doing and outsource the rest. Hate the idea of admin? Hire a VA (a virtual assistant) to help you. Taxes hurting your head? Hire a good accountant. Yes, it's a cost, and you might want to keep costs down as much as possible (especially in your early days), but often with these types of things, it'll save you time and money in the long run.

Sticking with the accountant example, a good accountant might charge a few hundred pounds to do an annual tax return on your behalf. But what if you decided to go it alone and spent hours and hours trying to do it all yourself only to screw it up, when you could've spent that time doing a few hundred pounds-worth of billable client work instead? Worse yet, what if you miss a trick that an accountant could've helped you with, such as telling you that something is tax deductible that you wouldn't have known otherwise? And another unpleasant scenario: what if you screw it up so bad that you receive a fine from HMRC (the UK's tax department)? So, the alternative is to outsource that stuff to an expert, so that we, as freelancers, can concentrate on the core efforts of our business and line of work. Huzzah.

As practical as it is, this outsourcing scenario has a snag: it doesn't apply to sales. How do you outsource sales? You can't, really. I can't even begin to think about how you'd do it – at least not in its entirety, sadly. Even if you were to hire someone to help you to get leads, you still have to convert them. Even if you hire someone to help you to write proposals, you still have to decide what goes in them, including the type of work that's required. In other words, you still have to be involved with at least some part of the sales process: meeting the client, finding out what they need, delivering a proposal, deciding on a fee for services rendered, and so on. You can't really outsource that. Sorry guys...

For that reason, sales is the bane of the freelancing life. I just want to crack on and do the work that I enjoy doing, but in order to do that, I have to first sell my services to people. *Ack.*

What's worse is that sales as a whole is perceived to be a slimy, sleazy, slippery process. Do I have to don a suit? Do I have to go to business networking events, give people an elevator pitch, and slip a business card in their hands?

Argh! That's not me at all. And it might not be something that you relate to, either.

The good news is, that while you *can* sell yourself that way, it's not the only way.

In fact, I argue that you can sell yourself in a way that really isn't sales-y at all. It's about you being **you**: a good human being who helps out and imparts his or her knowledge to those in need.

The best way to sell is not to sell. Let that sink in. The

best way to sell is **not** to sell. It sounds completely and utterly counterintuitive, but it's the truth. Hence the name of this book: *Anti-Sell*. And in this book, I'll tell you how and why it works, and how to do it.

Here's what this book has in store for you in the upcoming chapters:

In **Chapter 1**, for context, I'll briefly tell you my story, from how I started my career as an agency employee in early 2009, to taking the plunge and becoming a full-time freelancer in mid-2013, to how I survived and met clients and made friends all along the way. For a guy with near enough zero professional sales training, who was pretty much told by two previous employers that I was bad at sales, I seem to have done alright for myself. I've worked with more than fifty clients over five years and still receive a decent number of enquiries on both a regular and recurring basis – the majority of which I have to turn down a lot of the time as I'm almost always too busy, operating at full capacity. But don't worry, I'm not going to sell to you while I run through this chapter – that would be a major turn-off, right? ...BUY MY SEO SERVICES – hahaha just kidding...

In **Chapter 2,** I talk about the traditional salesperson. Are you picturing Alec Baldwin's character in

Glengarry Glen Ross yet? Don't worry if you don't know the character or the film off-hand – but I bet you the moment I start quoting his lines, you'll know *exactly* what I'm talking about. I go on to argue that the traditional view of the typical salesperson – whether that's in popular culture or even your experience in the workplace pre-freelancing – might be exactly what you're picturing when it comes to sales. But do not fear – it really doesn't have to be that way. Trust me.

In **Chapter 3**, I talk about the difference between outbound sales and inbound sales, which is whether you should go out and seek sales or let the sales come to you, respectively.

Chapter 4 dives into the real meat n' bones of the book – and in fact, it's the main inspiration for the book's existence: it gives a long list of sales, marketing, networking and lead generation tips that you might want to consider trying out for your freelancing business. The idea is that while not all of them will resonate with you (or even be feasible for you to carry out), the hope is that a few of them will tie in with your passions and your strengths. And it's at *that* point when stuff starts to get really exciting in your business...

Hot on the heels of Chapter 4, **Chapter 5** reiterates the

Anti-Sell Formula... What is it about the bucketload of tactics and ideas that I lay out in Chapter 4 that connects them all? What's the running theme throughout?

I appreciate a lot of Chapter 4 and 5 is easier said than done, so **Chapter 6** gives further advice if you consider yourself to fit a certain profile, such as considering yourself an introvert, or struggling to get stuff done because you have young kids (trust me, I know how that feels – I KNOW...), or consider yourself extremely sensitive, or have a chronic illness or disability.

In **Chapter 7**, I highlight and then hone in on one of the points that I made during Chapter 4: be semi-relevant, not entirely relevant. What do I mean here? Well, the best way to network isn't to go to industry events, it's to go to events in semi-related industries where you can get to know people who work closely on what you *don't* do (and vice versa). Be the only online marketer in a room full of web designers, for example.

Chapter 8 talks about going niche. The more niche you go, the more specialist you become, the better you're perceived to be in that specialism, and the easier you are to refer.

In **Chapter 9**, I talk about how you can find more of your good-fit clients – perhaps those more fitting of a niche that works well with you, if you take on-board the advice from Chapter 8. This is for the more established freelancer, i.e. someone who already has clients past and present, and can compare and contrast them against various scoring criteria in order to work out who are the best-fit (and, sadly, the worst-fit) clients.

In **Chapter 10**, I examine the stigma and outright untruth that freelancers can't effectively work with big clients, and that apparently only agencies are suitable to work with clients of such size, status and stature. Us freelancers have a lot of advantages against agencies when you sit down and take the time to analyse them all. Bigger doesn't automatically mean better, y'know.

In **Chapter 11**, I pass on my main tip for when acquiring testimonials from happy clients. It might seem obvious when you read it, and it might even be something you're doing already, but if not then you could be missing a trick.

In **Chapter 12**, I explain why employing Anti-Sell tactics – such as those laid out in Chapter 4 – might be the only marketing and networking you really need to do henceforth, and why it doesn't hurt to consider entering yourself into an award or two.

In **Chapter 13**, I tell you why keeping your cool is of the utmost importance at all times, digging from a personal story of a time when I was humiliated on stage in front of around a hundred people. But even so, in spite of that, it still led to a dream client referral – mainly because of the way that I handled the uncomfortable aftermath.

Chapter 14 is all about the f-word... No, not *that* f-word! The f-word that antagonises every freelancer I've ever known: "freebie." See also its close cousin: "favour." I talk about this most delicate of subjects, suggesting how you might want to tackle it when someone approaches you asking for advice, but you have a sneaking feeling that all they might want from you at this stage is a bit of free advice or work and nothing more.

In **Chapter 15**, I introduce 'the Brinley method,' inspired by a sales mentor I knew who recommended charting your progress. This might sound similar to what I covered back in Chapter 9, but it's a slightly different approach. This is all about charting your progress with your *prospects and enquiries* – not your clients – and figuring out what's working for you, and what isn't. Are speaking gigs getting you enquiries, or is it your podcasting efforts? Admittedly it's good to be visible in multiple areas, but you may not want to keep spending your time on an activity that, as it turns out, doesn't help your business' bottom line in the long run.

Chapter 16 covers generosity. When you're in a position where you're too busy to take on any additional client work, what do you do with those leads?

In **Chapter 17**, I talk about transitioning from being a freelancer to growing your own agency, should you wish to (you don't have to, by the way). I'm not especially qualified to talk about it too much because I haven't actually done it myself, so the angle I take with this chapter is about how you can take your Anti-Sell methods further – not just you, but your new employees too.

And finally, in the closing thoughts, I wrap it all up. There's also a list of other books I recommend for further reading.

Also, you will find a few Anti-Sell Stories interspersed between some of the chapters, where fellow freelancers and friends of mine contribute their experiences of doing some of the things that this book suggests and how it's helped them on their respective journeys.

To reiterate, before we get properly started: I'm not a salesperson. I'm certainly not a sales guru – a word so horrid that it makes me want to retch. I've had absolutely zero sales training, other than a couple of meetings with a business management consultant and a one-day workshop I sat in on a few years ago. This book runs through my story, my journey and my tactics on how I've managed to win work without selling myself too much (or selling my soul too much, for that matter). At heart, I'm a freelancer who does sales, not a salesperson.

For that reason, I guess this isn't a traditional sales book – heck, if it was, I very much doubt you would've even considered picking it up. In fact, I'd argue that seasoned sales executives might even hate this book. When asking friends and fellow business owners for their feedback and advice when I was writing it (some of whom are referenced in later chapters), I noticed that those who were new to freelancing or who struggled with sales really resonated with the idea of the book and its concepts. A few people said something along the lines of this: *"I love the idea of this book – I've been a salesperson for twenty years, so I bet I'll love it."*

Ironically, they probably *won't* love it. Why? Because it's not for them. It's not targeted to them and it's not meant for them. It's not a traditional sales book. In one way or another, I'd even go as far as to say that it isn't even a *sales* book. It turns the idea of sales on its head. Well, traditional sales anyway. It's not a book for salespeople; it's a book for regular freelancers and owners of small businesses who struggle with sales. Folk like you and me.

The book is heavily inspired by *ReWork*, the most rebellious business book I've ever read (and quite possibly my favourite business book of all time). It feels a little corny making a comparison and suggesting that this book is rebellious too, but hey – if you're a freelancer (or thinking of becoming one), then you're a rebel anyway. You've decided to ditch the traditional employee route to go it alone. That's incredibly brave, and rebellious as hell.

So, here's to us rebels. May you sell (or *not* sell) your way to a successful freelance business.

CHAPTER 1
A bit about me (don't worry, I'm not going to sell to you)

"You'll never last a day in self-employment."

Someone in a senior role at an old job said this to me when I mentioned that I'd been considering becoming a freelancer. Unfortunately, it didn't come across as playful banter or just to wind me up. To my ears, it sounded as though they meant it. I was just making conversation, saying that I was interested in going self-employed at some point in the future, so perhaps they were just being defensive with their remark. After all, I was an employee of theirs, and they probably didn't want to lose me.

However, whatever the thought was behind the comment, it had a galvanising effect: it made me want to become self-employed even more so, and I'm happy to say that – having been a freelancer now for over five years – that I've proved them wrong at least 1,825 times over.

There's a reason why the theme of this chapter runs through my story. When I first listened to the audiobook of Ben Horowitz's *The Hard Thing About Hard Things*, I liked it, but I wasn't completely convinced by it. But the second time I heard it, I realised something that made it snap into sharper focus. With most books and audiobooks, the author might talk a little bit about who they are and what they do throughout the book, but at the end of the day, they mostly just dole out advice. In Ben's case, he spends a good 50% or so of the book just telling his story. On the first listen, I found this a little boring... *"Why do I need to know anything about him? I just want the advice. Gimme the advice, goshdarnit!"* I didn't much care for hearing the guy's life story. But in the latter half of the book, when he *does* give advice, it hits a lot harder, as you realise that it's backed up by that been-there-done-that-and-survived mentality.

So I hope you don't mind if I take a leaf out of Ben's book and do the same. I'll keep it much shorter though, I promise.

I got into my career in SEO in early 2009. SEO stands for Search Engine Optimisation. In a nutshell, it's the process of improving a website's presence in search engines, such as Google. By doing so, said website gets more visitors, which may result in more ad revenue, or product sales, or enquiries, or whatever it is that helps the business attached to the website make more money. It was actually my older brother Gareth who introduced me to the wonderful world of SEO. He'd started an online marketing agency specialising in SEO, known as Liberty Marketing (or Liberty for short), and I was his first official hire.

For the first year that I was involved, it was just my brother and I. We didn't need an office; he worked from his house, and I worked from my house, and occasionally we'd meet up to catch up, discuss clients, and so on. It was my first ever work-from-home job, and for the first few months, the novelty of it was a luxury. You mean I can work my own hours, so I could take a weekday off and make it up on a Sunday? Or have a lie-in and work in the afternoon and evening instead? Or take a two-hour lunch break and play video games, so long as I make up that time elsewhere? And I can work in my pyjamas?! ...You get the idea at this point. However, surprisingly to me, the novelty wore off fairly quickly. Stuck in a house all day by myself with nobody to talk to (not counting the cats), it eventually grew quite lonely and isolating, and by the end of the year, I was entirely fed up with it.

You see, I did a lot of the 'grunt' work, to put it one way. Gareth met with the clients, went to networking groups, exhibited at events, and so on – so he was always socialising and meeting people. While I worked from my coffee table for 40 hours per week, every week. He did some of the work himself, sure, but passed a good number of tasks over to me to do.

Then in late 2009, we had enough client work going on that we needed another employee. We'd run out of brothers to hire (it was just him and me, after all), so we had to hire someone... well... a little less blood relative-y. We weren't looking to hire someone to work remotely (it wasn't as common back then as it is now), instead wanting to work with someone more closely. Asking them to work from either his or my house was out of the question too. This meant only one thing: it was time to get our own office space.

Soon after, employees started trickling in at a phenomenal rate – especially given the economic downturn which had hit just a couple of years earlier. I think we might've had five to six employees just another year later, as we were approaching the latter half of 2010. To keep the ball rolling, Gareth asked me to start going to networking events as well. He'd had a lot of success joining a BNI chapter and wanted me to join a different chapter so that I could get in on the action as well. BNI stands for Business Networking International, and is a global networking group with local branches (called 'chapters') that hold weekly meetings.

I wouldn't necessarily consider myself someone who's shy, but after working for 40 hours a week for a year in my own house, it was a miracle that I still knew how to conduct myself socially *and* professionally at all...! I was certainly a little intimidated by the idea, plus it didn't help that BNI meetings were held early in the mornings over breakfast, so you had to get there for 7am, if not earlier. Oof! A few years earlier, when I'd been a university student, I often didn't see *anything* before 10am. This was gonna hurt.

BNI has a mixed reputation, so much so that I often

joke that it's the Marmite of networking events: some people love it, some people despise it. Thankfully, I fell into the former category almost immediately. It was a good group of people, some of whom – nearly a decade later – are still good friends of mine.

Obviously, our goal at BNI was to get Liberty new clients, as well as to promote the agency's name locally. Going to BNI meetings worked really well for me, because Gareth asked me to pass on to him anyone who was interested in working with us. In other words, he'd take care of the sales bit, so all I had to do was network. And I loved it! I hated the idea of selling stuff (eurgh!) but I could easily and happily talk to people about my passion (SEO), listen to their struggles, offer them advice, and generally just chat with them about it. And hey, if it led to a referral, then even better!

After another year into my time at Liberty, a role came up at Confused.com, the well-known UK insurance price comparison website, whose head office is based in Cardiff, where I live. As it turned out, I didn't have the best experience there. I learnt a lot, but I joined at a very stressful and turbulent time at the company, with lots of staff changes and a major revamp of their website in-the-works. I was the only contractor in the twenty-or-so-strong marketing department at the time, and when the CEO was replaced and there was chatter of possible redundancies throughout the company, I knew I'd almost certainly get the chop, so I looked for another job right away. I ended up in another in-house role in South Wales, which I won't name because it was dreadful: I walked out after only three weeks and it doesn't appear on my CV or on my LinkedIn profile, and to this day only a handful of people know what company it was.

It was at this time that I considered going self-employed working solely on Local SEO, a specialised niche within SEO that involves optimising Google Maps listings for businesses that have a brick-and-mortar store or an office address. I had a knack for the work from my Liberty days, but it was unpopular work as it was quite difficult and frustrating, especially if there were problems. I met with Gareth to discuss a potential relationship whereby he'd pass me Local SEO work and I'd pass him anything else – so we'd be non-competing referral partners, despite both working in SEO – but the idea of self-employment terrified me at the time. So he said: *"why don't you just come back to Liberty instead?"* And so I did.

For another year and a half, I worked for Liberty at my second stint at the agency. When I'd returned in early 2011, we were at new premises and were probably up to a dozen employees. My old BNI chapter had since disbanded, so I joined a different one, which was also made up of a good group of people. I also got the chance to attend the twice-yearly conference, brightonSEO, with two of my colleagues. And I was also starting to get into attending social events and meetups, such as WordPress Users Wales and – my absolute favourite at the time – Cardiff Blogs. So in addition to BNI, I was networking all over the place and at different types of events.

I left Liberty for the second and final time during the summer of 2012. Instead of taking on an in-house role, I went to a web development agency that wanted to start a digital marketing department, and who typically worked with a different type of clients to those at Liberty.

I was at Box UK for about a year, and it was my last job before going self-employed. It was while I was working there that I was approached by a couple of people I knew asking if I was taking on any freelance work, such as taking on side-gigs during the evenings and weekends. I told them no. Box UK was busy enough for me, to be fair. They often replied by saying that if I ever went self-employed, they'd become a client of mine. At first this only happened once or twice, but as the months went by, I had about a dozen people say this to me. I did the maths and figured out that if only two or three of them converted and went on to become clients, it'd be a good start on a path of full-time freelancing. I gave my notice to Box UK, working my last ever day as an employee on Friday 3rd May 2013. The following Monday was a Bank Holiday, so from the following Tuesday, 7th May, I was officially self-employed.

I was so thrilled and hugely excited to be starting my own business. I absolutely knew I could do it, but there was one big problem: I had to do sales, and worse, I had to do all sales all by myself! Sales. *Sales*! My one weakness. My Achilles heel! Various people at both Liberty and Box UK had hinted that while I was good at SEO, and even good at networking, I was terrible at sales – which was probably what lay behind the quote at the beginning of this chapter, that I *"wouldn't last a day in self-employment."* I knew I could do the work, and I knew I could meet potential clients, but could I get any of them on-board...?

Straight away I revisited the list of the dozen or so people who said they'd work with me if I ever went freelance. Unfortunately, for most of them, their situations had changed: they were now already working with another freelance SEO consultant or an SEO agency, or they didn't have the budget for it anymore, or they had moved on and were working for a different company now. Of the dozen or so people who, once upon a time, I considered prospective clients, only **one** actually became a client. Our arrangement was only a small monthly retainer, certainly not something that was going to cover all the bills (although I'm proud to say that over five years on, that monthly retainer is still going).

I knew I needed to ramp up my efforts – and fast. One of my biggest regrets was not doing the more sensible thing of carrying out a bit of freelance work *while still at* Box UK, and then transitioning to full-time freelancing once I had three or more clients, or one big juicy one. But what's done is done, and now I warn others not to make the same mistake that I once made if they have the opportunity to ease into self-employment.

It took three or four months, but things did start to pick up. After delving into my savings and dealing with upfront costs – such as getting company branding, business cards, a new website, and so on – I broke-even by Month 3. I think it was by about Month 6 that I reached full capacity status for the first time, whereby my workload was full and I couldn't accept any more additional work. Many other freelancers that I know seemed to hit those milestones much quicker than I did. But at the same time, I know some who struggled even more than I did, so I should be grateful for my achievements back then (and I am).

To win business in the early days of my new freelancing life, I stuck to what I knew, which was BNI. Rather than select and join a chapter straight away, I took the time to visit multiple chapters, in order to check each of them out. I don't know if this is still the case today, but back then you were only allowed to visit a chapter twice within a six-month period without having to make a commitment to join. So I visited about four or five different chapters, visiting each of them twice for two weeks in a row. It was a *knackering* couple of weeks, I'll say that much! The BNI ethos is that in order to get the most out of it, you should really commit to one chapter for as long as possible. While my method was the exact reverse of this (i.e. only visiting each chapter briefly as a one-off), it was a great way to get business cards out and to get 'word on the street' that I was now a solo freelancer, as some people already knew me but only in the context of being an agency employee. Even so, I still managed to land a new client or two out of the experience, which was good.

Another method that worked well for me was joining a coworking space. People who know me through Twitter (perhaps before buying this book) will probably already know that I'm a member of Welsh ICE, a coworking space in Caerphilly, a town just outside of Cardiff. I say you'll *"know that I'm a member"* because I love Welsh ICE and often won't shut up about it! While I was only looking for somewhere where I could have a desk, WiFi and coffee, and to get out of my house (as there was no way in hell I was gonna fall into that trap of loneliness again!), being at ICE also resulted in some work, because fellow members asked me for help with their SEO.

Other clients came from word of mouth, and as referrals from other people that I knew. One prospect said he'd read my blog – SEOno, which I started in 2011, while still at my second stint at Liberty – and was impressed with my posts so much that he wanted to work with me as a result. Some people (rather fittingly) found me through Google, when using keywords such as "seo cardiff" and "online marketing cardiff". Others discovered me through the meetups I attended, such as Cardiff Blogs.

Over the years, I've had a steady stream of work come through, and eventually achieved having only retainer clients on my plate. Ongoing retainers are a much better situation than working on lots of one-off projects because with one-off work, you have to juggle the tasks alongside constantly needing to fill your sales funnel ready for when your current workload finishes. The beauty of the ongoing retainer is that you fulfil the monthly commitment, and you know how much you're going to earn that month and the next – and if one client gives you 30 days' notice, it's much easier to fill the gap because you may only have to replace it with one other client of equal size and value.

The golden rule is to ask prospects this: *"how did you find me?"* I discovered that other ways I had won work had included guest blogging, whereby you write a blog post and offer it to another blog to publish; speaking gigs at local meetups (I remember how one speaking gig in front of only fifty attendees resulted in at least half a dozen enquiries afterwards – I'll talk more about that in a later chapter); and more recently, running my own meetup – Cardiff SEO Meet – and getting to know prospective clients when they come to the events.

I still work for myself and by myself, although it is feasible for me to grow my business, Morgan Online Marketing, into an agency. The only reason I haven't just yet is because I have two young kids, and I know that if I start growing an agency, I won't get to spend much time with them. So when I hit that capacity ceiling, I have to turn the work away, or pass it on to one of a number of friends who also offer freelance SEO services and who I trust will do a good job in my place. Perhaps the 'busiest' month in terms of the number of enquiries I received was in January 2018, when I received on average a new enquiry **every business day** during the month – that's about **twenty** enquiries in one month. But I was already at full capacity at the time, so I turned them all away. Where were all these guys in my first few months of freelancing, huh?! Typical, eh?

Since starting over five years ago, I've had more than fifty paying clients (some as one-off projects, some as monthly retainers). And I've also had to sell sponsorship of my SEO meetup – Cardiff SEO Meet – as the event has a number of sponsorship slots in order to cover the cost of the food and drink at each event, as well as other things that help to keep the event running smoothly.

Not bad for someone who hates sales (I still do, by the way) and who was pretty much told by two previous employers that I sucked at sales.

So what's the point of me telling you this long-winded story of five to ten years of my life in 3,000 or so words? The reason is that despite being terrified of the idea of going self-employed and despite hating sales, I was able to do it. If anything, the opposite is now happening, and I have more enquiries than I can handle – a nice problem to have, admittedly. I wouldn't exactly call myself a sales guru (bleeeugh!) but I'm proof that I have been able to sell effectively, despite always considering sales to be one of my weakest qualities.

So if anyone tells you that you suck at sales, or that you *wouldn't last a day in self-employment,"* don't believe them for a second. Prove them wrong, just as I did. Like I said earlier, I've proved that person wrong every day for five years. That's over 1,825 days.

Here's to at least another 1,825 more.

CHAPTER 2
The Typical Salesperson: Why do we Hate Selling Ourselves so much?

Freelance Heroes is a private Facebook group with over 5,000 members, as I write this. It's a popular group where freelancers leave questions for others to jump in and assist with. Every week, they run a 'Monday Poll,' and in October 2018, they ran one that asked the following question: *"Which area of your freelance business are you least skilful at, and probably enjoy less as a result?"* The highest answer – 55% of the participants – answered: *"finding new leads."* For the record, the next three highest-rated options were *"bookkeeping," "social media"* and *"credit control"* – so at 55%, *"finding new leads"* beat all those (and others)

combined. Another similar poll in August 2018 asked: *"in the last three months, what has been [your] biggest challenge?"* Again, *"Finding new customers"* came out on top, with 51% of the vote.

But why do we find sales so challenging, so intimidating and so unenjoyable? I discovered that one of the reasons I didn't love sales was because I couldn't identify with its image. Picture this scene...

A man in a suit stands in front of a chalkboard, talking – and even yelling – at a few other men sat at desks. He says a few motivational wisecracks, such as *"A B C = Always Be Closing"* and *"coffee is for closers!"* He comes across as someone senior to them, someone who knows what they're doing and speaks from a position which suggests that if the men don't work hard enough, they're done for.

...Are you picturing Alec Baldwin yet?

The scene I'm talking about is from the movie *Glengarry Glen Ross* and it has gone on to represent the quintessential salesperson and the quintessential sales process. That is:

- Someone who's a fast-talker, a wise-cracker, a schmoozer, a seller,

- Someone who aggressively pursues the sale, like a shark pursuing its next meal,
- Someone who can't fail – because if they do, they're outta there.

Thanks to this movie and scenes like it in popular culture (think *Jerry Maguire, Boiler Room, The Pursuit of Happyness* and, far more recently, *The Wolf of Wall Street*), sales is seen to be this dodgy, sleazy, non-reputable process where salespeople only care about making the sale, no matter the cost – even if it ends up in a bad experience for the customer. As a result, people often turn their nose up at the idea of sales and I bet there are a good few budding freelancers out there who'd love the idea of freelancing but are put off by having to do the sales-y bit, similar to how I felt when I first started out.

The danger of being exposed to such instances of popular culture (or even people like this directly, if you've worked in an agency environment) is that it *reinforces the idea* that the sales process and salespeople have to be ruthless, brash and ballsy – three words I would **never** use to describe myself personally, hah! You might not use those words to describe yourself, either.

But it doesn't have to be this way. In fact it *isn't* this way at all, not in the slightest.

You *don't* have to be like that. The best thing about sales as a freelancer is that you can be **you**, and it should all still work out (so long as "**you**" isn't a complete jerk scumbag, of course – you have to have *some* social etiquette, if only a little).

What I'm saying is that you don't have to be ruthless, brash or ballsy, or pushy, or extroverted, or whatever other words you might have swimming around in your head when you're asked to describe a salesperson.

You can just be you.

In the rest of this book, I'll give you tips on how you can achieve just that. But for now, feel free to breathe a big sigh of relief that you don't have to delay your coffee until you've made a sale today. Feel free to make one now if you want. I'll wait.

...

Dum-de-dum...

...

Whistles

...

...

Looks at watch

...

Oh, you're back? Good. Let's continue...

CHAPTER 3
The Death of (Outbound) Sales

In addition to the thoughts we may have about salespeople, another sales concern to freelancers can be the processes and tasks involved.

In order to sell, we have to contact, meet and get to know people. And in order to contact, meet and get to know people, we have to see people, or call people, or email people. This process is generally referred to as *outbound* sales: the process of getting in touch with someone who may or may not already know you, and – worse still – may or may not even want or need your services, whether at that moment in time (or ever)!

Think cold-calling or cold-emailing. If anyone has ever bought a web domain and not hidden their WHOIS info (the information associated with a domain that can be accessed publicly, which may contain your postal address, email address and phone number), you'll have no doubt been inundated by junk emails from people trying to sell you web design, online marketing and (gasp!) SEO services. It makes sense for these uninvited businesses to contact you when they do – after all, you've just bought a domain, so you probably need a website and some online marketing to go with it – but I don't know a single person who hasn't been annoyed by being contacted in this way, let alone anyone who has ever taken up their offer and hired them or their services as a result.

Let's say a random person – let's call her Rachel – is in need of a website, having just bought a web domain. What would she do next? She'd probably ask her friends or family for recommendations, right? Or if she already knew of a great web designer with an excellent reputation, she may contact him or her directly. Or failing that, she might use a search engine to see who's local to her.

The difference between the two situations is that Rachel is the one controlling the process. She's the one who's in need of a website at that exact moment in time – and chances are, she'd rather work with someone who comes highly recommended, or that she's heavily researched prior to contacting them, rather than the first randomer who happens to approach her.

Sticking with this example, where it's Rachel who contacts the web designer, the process is known as *inbound* sales for the web designer. The prospective client has contacted *them* - not the other way around. The web designer knows that she needs a website right now or soon, rather than he or she contacting Rachel at a random time that will probably not be convenient to her.

This situation is the perfect way for sales to be made. The only challenge posed is that you're reliant on people finding you, rather than you pestering people at a time when your workload is quiet. If, say, you perform outbound sales activities and contact fifty people right now, maybe one will reply who'll want to know more (and in doing so, you might have annoyed the other forty-nine, potentially damaging your reputation in the process). But if you only practice inbound sales, it's impossible to control or guarantee how and when prospective clients will contact you. Sure, you could go to a meetup event to network, which may result in an enquiry or two – but of course, it may not. However, in my experience (as someone who's never invested any time or money into outbound sales for my freelance business), inbound sales are a much better, much smoother and less painful process. Especially when that tipping point is hit, with lots of people making contact expressing interest in working with you, which has happened to me a few times over the years.

But what can you actually do to influence the situation? What methods, tools and tactics can be used to improve your inbound sales? Well, for a few ideas of where to get started, let's turn over to Chapter 4...

CHAPTER 4
The Long List of Marketing, Networking and Lead Generation Tactics

The idea for this book came from a years-old blog post I'd written. I'd just come through a quiet spell on the work front – I'm fortunate to say that I've only ever had two such spells during my five-year-plus freelance career, the first one of which was when I'd first started out. In the second instance, in early 2015, I was caught up in two big projects and was too busy to meet with any prospective clients or to get any proposals out to anyone. Then, when those big projects came to an end, and I realised I had very little work on, I had that classic "...*oh*" moment. I needed to get me some sales.

It took a while to get things back up to full capacity

again (probably a couple of months), after which I had the idea to write down a number of the things I did to try and stave off the work drought. I published it on SEOno, which is my SEO blog (I say "SEO blog," but it's sort of a publish-whatever-the-heck-I-want blog – there's been posts about self-employment and freelancing, coworking life, social media marketing, and even music… it's a whole mixed bag).

The original list had twenty ideas – this chapter contains some of them plus a few more. The whole point is to arm you with a ridiculously long list of ideas for sales, marketing, lead generation and networking tactics for you to choose from. You're not expected to implement them all – although hey, if you do try out every single one, you would deserve some sort of prize, 'cos that would most certainly be impressive! The idea is that you try the suggestions that resonate the most with you. Hopefully there'll be at least one or two you see as having potential as you work your way through the list, if not more.

I remember working with a client once and recommending blogging as an SEO tactic. I suggested to him that he could write blog posts that could later be found when people Googled what he'd written about.

He stopped me there, saying: *"Sorry Steve, I don't like writing."* As my heart began to sink, he said: *"...but I do like making videos; is that any good?"* Foolishly, I hadn't thought about his background working in TV and film production. I told him that videos were indeed another tactic we could try, and better yet, it'd be working to his strengths and past experience. So why have I included this anecdote? Because I want you to do the same. When you go through this list, think about whether the tactic you're perusing is something you'd like to do, or something you know that you can do particularly well. Having two or three things that fit that profile will put you in better stead than randomly trying half a dozen tactics that do not.

I must admit though that while some of these tactics worked for me at that lean time, some have continued to help me more recently as well. A few I haven't even tried, but I know they've worked for others. You'll notice a 'theme' developing too, as I go through them – and admittedly some do overlap, or are essentially the same thing as something previously suggested but done in a slightly different format.

Before we get stuck in, and I probably shouldn't have to say this, but there is a quick disclaimer: you will not find a 'silver bullet' strategy anywhere here. There's no cheat code or magic wand-waving way to activate floods of enquiries or an easier sales process. There's none of that 'get rich quick' type of stuff here at all, I'm afraid. Sorry about that (but I'm guessing you probably knew that already). Some of these tactics may involve a bit of work to get them going and then maintain them, but like I said a paragraph or so ago, it is possible to tie it in with what you love and enjoy doing, to the point where it won't even feel like work – or sales. So there's that at least.

Anyway, let's get to business (err, no pun intended)...

Go to Business Networking Events

Let's get the obvious one out of the way first, although typically, it's probably the one you're *least* likely to want to do...

As mentioned in Chapter 2, I used to frequent BNI, a formal business networking group. You meet with other business owners or salespeople and try to refer work to each other. Each chapter abides by a 'one person per profession' rule, so I'd be the only SEO allowed in the group, and consequently, there might only be one plumber, one florist, one car dealership representative, one graphic designer, and so on. This rule was intended to avoid the awkwardness of not knowing who to give a referral to if, for instance, you know someone who needs SEO help but there are two different SEO companies in the room. It's also good for people who feel a little threatened when their competitors are at the same networking event as them.

There are plenty of other business networking groups out there, with some similar to BNI, and others that differ a lot. 4Networking (known as 4N) was one that was similar to BNI, which I believe didn't follow the 'one person per profession' rule (I never went to it, but I did hear good things about it from others). There might also be local independent ones: for example, in Newport (a city near Cardiff, where I live) there's Action Business Club (known as ABC for short), a one-off group which started out as a few people from the same BNI chapter who decided to run their own thing, in their own way instead. And other types, such as women-only networking events: for example, Re:Program is a Cardiff-based networking group for women who work in tech, digital and entrepreneurship.

It's worth trying out different business networking events to see what works for you and what doesn't. It's also important to bear in mind that it's the *people* there who make or break a particular group. You might go to one BNI chapter and find it a bad fit, but then go to another one and get along with everyone really well. However, most people I know would probably stop attending after an initial negative experience and end up thinking that BNI just isn't for them at all. That's probably not the case, so I'd recommend trying two or three different chapters and 'types' of business networking events, because many of them are run in different ways. For example, BNI is quite structured and they require a regular commitment and following a strict agenda, while at the other end of the spectrum, another business networking group might be agendaless, so you can just go along and chat to the other people who are in the room.

Go to Meetups

If business networking groups aren't necessarily your thing, you may prefer to go to a meetup instead. While these still revolve around work (at least in topic), they tend to be more informal and social, and therefore more of a learning opportunity. For example, a couple of meetups close to where I live include unified.diff, which specialises in web and software development; and Cardiff Blogs, which specialises in blogging. There's usually a few talks or lectures on a topic and often some good networking opportunities (the latter of which is often overlooked or ignored but is an added benefit of going). If you're not sure where to look for meetups in your area, a good starting point is to use the website Meetup.com.

I find that people who are uncomfortable in formal business networking settings such as BNI, might find that they do much better networking-wise at a meetup. So if this resonates with you, then treat meetups as your preferred way to network. Just because business networking events have "business" in the name and meetups are often considered to be more social and informal, it doesn't mean to say that business networking events are the gold standard. They're not. There's nothing wrong with networking at meetups instead. And besides, you may find that you get just as many referrals, or possibly even more.

My golden tip? Don't just go to the meetup that's most closely related to what you do for a living, otherwise you'll simply surround yourself with all your industry peers and competitors. Go to other semi-related meetups as well. So if you're a web designer for example, don't just go to a web design meetup – consider going to a software developer meetup, or a blogger meetup, or an SEO meetup. You might be the only person who does what you do in a room full of potential referral partners. This technique has worked wonders for me. If I'm the only SEO who shows up to an event full of web developers – some of whom may not even know any other SEO professionals – then who are they going to refer SEO work to the next time they come across someone who needs help with SEO? This guy right here! (You can't see this because it's a book, but I just pointed at myself with both thumbs.)

Run a Meetup

Want to take the meetups tip up a notch? Don't just go to meetups – **run** a meetup, whether as part of a team or all on your own. I do the latter with Cardiff SEO

Meet, and while it does require a fair bit of effort on an ongoing basis, it's resulted in a few really good enquiries, including one dream client. I probably wouldn't have met them if they hadn't come to my events and gotten to know me that way.

Want to know something interesting? Being an event organiser conveys the perception that you are an expert in your industry – perhaps one of the best. I discovered this first-hand when I used to attend the events of a guy I know: the more I went along to his events, and heard the great speakers he had personally selected, the more I considered him the best brain in his industry, hands down. But when I finally had the opportunity to work with him, I was disappointed to discover that his actual skill-level and quality of work weren't as high as I was expecting. Don't get me wrong, he was still very good at his trade and a highly switched-on guy, but admittedly I was expecting god-like levels of ability! So if you like the idea of running events and want to get onto the radar of people and maybe be seen as the authority of your industry on a local scale, then I recommend this tactic – even if it does feel a bit weird and dodgy to be saying: *"you don't have to be the best in your industry to be seen as the best."* It really is true, though.

Take Part in Webinars

Don't necessarily like the idea of meeting people face-to-face? Why not participate in a webinar instead, such as those hosted on Google+ Hangouts On Air and other similar platforms?

Years ago I used to take part in Max Impact, a series of digital marketing webinars run on Google+ Hangouts On Air, hosted by Seattle-based SEO consultant Max Minzer. They each lasted around an hour, and they were a good way to discuss a topic and share ideas. I got to meet some great people and learnt a lot from them in the process.

For me, it didn't really lead to many referrals – although for one episode I was the special guest and was interviewed about a topic, which was a good brand-building exercise. However one of the other participants – Steve Webb, a US-based consultant who we referred to as 'US Steve' because I was also called Steve (naturally I was known as 'UK Steve') – was an SEO who hyper-specialised in an area of SEO known as 'technical SEO,' which is the process of tweaking the code and build of a website to help it to rank better. To my knowledge, he didn't touch any other areas of SEO: so no keywords, no links, no Google Map optimisation, or anything like that. This meant that anyone who didn't do technical SEO or who was struggling with it would go to him. And I'm pretty sure he got a few referrals thanks to his time spent on Max Impact.

Admittedly, not much happens on Google+ or Hangouts anymore, which likely will have been a contributory factor behind Google's pending decision to close the platform, so you may have to look around and see what's more readily available these days webinar-wise. It's also important to note that what made Max Impact stand out was the fact that Max let up to ten people join each session (it didn't matter who they were), so you could join in and contribute directly – and if it reached full capacity then people could still contribute by leaving comments on the accompanying Google+ or YouTube page. However some webinars are run so that only the host and the guest (or guests) are present in the webinar itself. Obviously if you're able to find a webinar of the former nature – where you can contribute directly, even if you're not that episode's special guest – then this would be a better way of getting known by the other attendees.

Run a Webinar

Remember my 'Run a Meetup' point a few sections ago? The same applies to webinars. Run your own webinar and be seen as an authority on the subject that you are presenting.

Run a Podcast

Are you starting to see the pattern now? If you run your own podcast – similar to if you were to run your own event or webinar – you get an additional boost in visibility.

I haven't included a 'Take Part in Podcasts' subsection – unlike the webinar tactic mentioned previously – because you can't really take part in one on the fly, given that they're often pre-recorded and therefore not run live. This is of course unless you were invited to speak on one. Which leads me nicely onto...

Speak at Meetups, Conferences, Events, and on Webinars and Podcasts

If you *really* want to ramp up the 'credibility-o-meter' then don't just go to events and meetups or jump in on the occasional webinar. Offer to speak at/on them.

My golden tip from a few sections ago also works well here: don't just speak at events that 100% match your industry – speak at semi-related events, those that complement and fit nicely, alongside your line of work.

It was an honour to speak at brightonSEO, the twice-yearly SEO conference in Brighton, UK. I spoke there twice: April 2015 and September 2016. However, despite it being a mighty big badge of honour and prestige within the industry, it only resulted in one enquiry – mainly because I was just passing on my knowledge to fellow SEOs, most of whom would probably be considered competitors more than anything. Admittedly, both times I presented on smaller stages, not the main stage, but still... there were probably 100-200 people in attendance each time that I spoke.

Compare that to the time I spoke at a local web

developer meetup of just fifty attendees. I think I had about half a dozen enquiries the following day, all of whom mentioned that they saw my talk and wanted to work with me as a result. *(Note: I don't mean "just fifty" derogatorily by the way – it's a good turnout for a local meetup, and the venue had a capacity of fifty, so it was considered a sell-out event.)*

So, let's do the maths here: one enquiry after speaking in front of hundreds of people at a big SEO event (twice), but half a dozen enquiries following my talk in front of fifty people at a small local web developer meetup. Such a difference.

The difference is because the latter was a semi-related event. I was an SEO talking to a room of web developers, presenting on a subject important to web developers but that isn't their main area of focus. I might've been the only SEO doing an SEO-related talk to the meetup's community all that year. Some of the audience might not know anyone else doing SEO. So who are they going to pass their enquiries to, or hire as a helping hand?

I love speaking at SEO events, don't get me wrong – but if you want to get enquiries from your speaking gig efforts then this is the way to go about it. I've also spoken at meetups that focused on ecommerce, PR, design and even a dedicated WordPress meetup, most (if not all) of which have resulted in enquiries: some straight away, some months or even years later.

In fact, the designer meetup – which was one of my least enjoyable experiences at a speaking gig – surprisingly led to one of the best enquiries I'd ever had a year or two later. I'll explain what happened in more detail in Chapter 13, when I talk about 'keeping your cool' and how bad experiences can still lead to great opportunities.

Depending on what you do for a living, you should be able to find opportunities for you as well. There are usually a few meetups of various types in towns and cities all across the UK and beyond. Other types of meetups might include social media meetups, blogger meetups, writer meetups, entrepreneurship meetups and many more. Whatever they specialise in, can you offer your expertise to them?

Join and Participate in Online Communities

Not everyone is happy or comfortable going out to meetups and events all the time, or it might be a struggle to do so. I've struggled ever since starting a family, as it's not as easy saying: *"right, I'm off to this meetup tonight"* when you have to give baby its bath, bottle and bedtime...

If you can't physically go out to network with groups of people at events, there's nothing stopping you from whipping out your laptop or smartphone and contributing online instead. Online spaces such as forums and Facebook groups are a great way to participate, get recognised and eventually win enquiries.

I put a lot of effort into two Facebook groups. The first one is Welsh ICE members' group, which is the private Facebook group for my coworking space (I'll talk about the joys of joining a coworking space later). The second one is Cardiff Start, a public Facebook group dedicated to the city's entrepreneurship and startup scene.

Cardiff Start has been especially fantastic for me,

networking-wise. While they have a strict 'no self-promotion' policy, and jumping on a thread saying *"hey, I'm a freelancer, hire me!"* is heavily frowned upon, helping people out is encouraged if, say, someone asks for SEO help. By chiming in with my thoughts and advice, I'm not directly selling myself – I'm just helping out, as any other SEO expert on there would do too. But in a way (as long as the advice is good and legit, of course), you *are* selling yourself, insofar as you're showing off your knowledge and expertise.

Having become known by the Cardiff Start community over the years, it's gotten to the point where if someone asks the group for a recommendation of a locally-based SEO professional, I'm often name-dropped and tagged in the conversation.

Run an Online Community

Yep, here I go again with a 'Run a [Something]' suggestion!

Be warned though; like with the suggestions above, running an online community can be a lot of hard work. Although running events, webinars and podcasts obviously takes a lot of work, running an online community might seem easier when in fact, oftentimes, it's a lot harder. You're just setting up a group and letting it run itself, right? Not necessarily. Depending how big the group gets, there can be a lot of admin, moderating and fire-fighting involved. The guys who run Cardiff Start can testify to that.

Participate in Twitter chats

By "Twitter chats" I don't just mean randomly chatting to people on Twitter (I mean, heck, do that anyway if you want), but what I specifically mean are those multi-participant chats that hover around a hashtag, and that usually last an hour long. #BlogHour – run by the UK Blog Awards – is an example, which I have contributed to on-and-off in the past. On Tuesdays from 9-10pm UK time, they'll ask a few questions such as *"What inspired you to start blogging?"* or *"What's your number one tip for having an effective blog homepage?"* or *"When working with brands, what questions do you tend to ask them?"* and so on, and Twitter users – typically other bloggers – can respond with their tips and advice.

Sometimes these chats follow a theme, so while one week might be quite generic, the following week may have questions that revolve around fashion blogging or using WordPress as a blogging platform, or another week might be about advertising on your blog, and so on. I remember one week being dedicated to SEO, so I had fun with that one!

With the #BlogHour example, while it's mostly bloggers and small business owners who contribute, I might be one of only a few SEOs who get involved, typically putting an SEO spin on the answers. So if it's a question about an ideal length of a blog post, I might chip in about the SEO effect of having a particularly long or short blog post, which might be something that the bloggers reading the tweet might not have thought about otherwise.

I recommend perusing the specific hashtags, then responding to other contributors directly as well, if applicable. An example might be if someone were to say: *"but I thought blog posts should always be x words in length"* – I could respond to them directly and offer my advice. In other words, don't just respond to the main set of questions and that's it, because you might miss out on further opportunities to answer other questions and help people.

Previously, I've had a couple of enquiries from people who have discovered me via my participation on #BlogHour and other similar chats. I remember one of them being quite a sizeable London-based company, so it's not necessarily the case that it'd just be bloggers (with potentially low budgets) getting in touch.

One tip for engaging in Twitter chats: don't be overly self-promotional. I see this a lot with this type of activity – people will just go on and share their blog posts, or say: *"hire me and I'll help you!"* Give advice and win admiration (and work) that way instead. I'm even reluctant to say: *"here's a blog post on the subject: [link],"* even if it'll genuinely help the person I'm tweeting it to, because it instantly looks like my ulterior motive was just to get people reading my content.

There are also Twitter chats that are location focused, such as #CardiffHour or #PortHour (the latter for Newport, a city near Cardiff), but be wary of those. Quite often you find that the ones that don't have a clear focus are just an excuse to tweet about your services, entirely self-promotionally. Imagine a room of a hundred people and each of them has a megaphone... it's a bit like that; people promoting themselves, but (quite likely, I would imagine) not actually wanting to hire the services of others doing the exact same thing on the hashtag. I might be wrong here, and I'm sure some people have benefitted from getting involved in them, but in my experience, the Twitter chats with a topic or industry focus that commit to a Q&A style structure are the best way to go here.

Run your own Twitter chat

Yep, there I go again... #sorrynotsorry

Join a Coworking Space

I love coworking – I'm a massive advocate of it. When I considered coworking many years ago, all I ever wanted was a desk, coffee and WiFi, and somewhere away from the distractions of home. But people often forget that it's also an incredible opportunity to get to know other freelancers, startups and small businesses – and to network, collaborate with and work with those businesses.

As mentioned in my intro, I'm a full-time member of Welsh ICE (a.k.a. the Welsh Innovation Centre for Enterprise), a successful coworking space in Caerphilly, a town situated just outside Cardiff. A good number of businesses based at ICE – and even ICE itself! – have become clients of mine over the years. And even for those that don't, I might be the only SEO person they know, so they'll refer me on to people who might be looking for SEO help. Would I have benefitted in this way if I'd worked from home all day, every day? Nope, probably not.

I also like to visit other coworking spaces – those that allow a 'pay for the day' type arrangement, where you can pop in and use their facilities on a one-off basis, sometimes also known as 'hot-desking'. This is particularly handy if I have meetings or errands to run in Cardiff city centre or Cardiff Bay, both of which are home to multiple coworking spaces: indycube, Tramshed Tech, Cardiff Eagle Lab, the Sustainable Studio and Rabble Studio, to name just a few. I'll pay for the day and use it as a base, fitting work around what else I need to do that day. Thanks to my networking habits over the years, I tend to know at least one or two people at each space, so it's a great opportunity to say hi and have a catch-up while I'm at it.

I appreciate that coworking isn't for everyone – some people find it too noisy and too distracting. Or on the other hand, if you work in an industry that's very heavy on the phone use, you may feel self-conscious about making too many calls around your coworkers, which is fair enough. A workaround for this might be to take a small office in a business centre that also has a coworking area, so that you can still mingle and network while also having a space of your own, just off to the side. Heck, depending on how quiet the coworking space is and how lenient the coworking manager is, you might be able to plonk your laptop down and work in the coworking area when you're not making phone calls (or not needing to be in your dedicated office) and jump back into your office as-and-when you need to, allowing you to chat and network with others during the time that you're in the coworking area. Best of both worlds.

Worried about it being an unnecessary cost, when you could just work from home instead? That's a fair concern. Some coworking spaces offer different price tiers and packages, one of which might be that you can hot-desk a few days per week or per month at a much lower rate than if you were based there full-time. You may not have a permanent desk there, but it's better than nothing. This arrangement can be especially handy if your job means you're on the road a lot, or if you still fancy working from home for some or most of the time. Some coworking spaces even offer funding deals. I was lucky at Welsh ICE to have my desk for free for the first year, a special deal they could offer as part of a Welsh Government funding initiative. By Year 2, finances are generally better in one's business than during Year 1, so the thinking behind it is to support entrepreneurs and freelancers in their first year in business but with the longer-term goal that they can hopefully afford the ongoing desk or office rental fee of their own accord from the thirteenth month onwards.

It's also important to note that it's the *people* that make a coworking space what it is. I made this same point when talking about business networking groups earlier, and it's the same principle here: try different coworking spaces and see which one is right for you – don't just join the very first one you come across, or the one that's closest to your home or with the easiest commute. Some offer free trials, so it's worth making use of them. You might find that the first coworking space you try out isn't the best fit, but the next one is your new 'forever home'...

You'll notice that I've not included a 'Run a Coworking Space' subsection this time. That's because running a coworking space is pretty much a full-time job. Seriously. If you want to run a coworking space then by all means run a coworking space. But if you want to be a freelancer or run a business as your primary source of income and you've had the idea to create a coworking space as a way to get a side-income, then let me stop you right now and suggest you reconsider. I know people who have done this and have then had to either close the coworking space (as it was too much of a distraction from their main business) or who have ended up heavily reducing the focus on their main business in order to let the coworking side of things take precedence. Another guy I know sold off his coworking space and even relocated his business so that he could be free of it entirely! If you have an office and want to sublet a desk or two, then that's fine I guess – but bear in mind that if your tenants have any issues with their Internet connection, the printer, the kettle, the coffee machine, etc., then you'll have to drop everything to help them there and then. And if you're in the middle of an important project for a client – and working to a deadline – then that's really not what you need. So, while I would encourage you to consider running an event, a webinar or something similar that you can fit around your daily activities, I advise that you proceed with caution if you are considering creating your own coworking space, or subletting some of your spare desks to other businesses. The whole thing can be an enormous time-suck.

Blog

I have a lot of love for blogging, mainly because I've been doing it for years and have (almost) always loved doing it. It's a great way to share what you're passionate about and to get things off your chest, all while showing off your expertise in the process. You might think *"why bother?"* but I've had a fair few enquiries from people as a result of my blogging efforts – not just from an individual blog post that might tackle a certain subject in depth, but from people saying: *"I've been following your blog for a while, and would like to work with you."*

I started SEOno in April 2011 and have tried committing to at least one new blog post per month – although admittedly I've let that slide a bit during the last couple of years, and these days I blog less about SEO and more about freelancing, running events and other random stuff... but hey, whatcha gonna do? It's my blog, so I can write about whatever I fancy.

Other added benefits to blogging include learning how to create and run your own website. I started my career in SEO in 2009 but started my blog two years later in 2011, and learnt a lot more about SEO from the experience of running my own website, by trying to get my own content to rank, playing around with the site's settings, running tests and experiments – stuff like that. If you're a designer, it's a way to learn a bit more (and show off about) design. If you're a writer, well... that one's obvious. But you get the idea.

Guest Blog

Whether or not you have your own blog already (or plan to start one), you can also write posts for other blogs as well or instead. Years ago, guest blogging was a very popular SEO tactic, because you would (or should) get a link back to your own website or blog in the process, which should help its SEO a bit – so SEOs (like me) used to do it for ourselves and on behalf of our clients. It's less popular now (it didn't help that a popular Google engineer at the time said that the tactic was 'overdone'), but despite that, it's still something to consider – and I'd argue that it's still a worthwhile tactic regardless.

A few years back, I contributed posts to a variety of different outlets. I would write one-off posts for sites and blogs such as Point Blank SEO, Koozai, Recruitment Buzz, SEMrush, Daily SEO Tip, TestLodge, Cardiff Start, Welsh ICE and – rather fittingly – MyBlogGuest, a resource that helped people find guest blogging opportunities, which had its own blog, which I guest blogged for... yep, that sentence hurt my head when I typed it just then, I won't lie.

I also contributed multiple times to two sites in particular: Moz and State of Digital. Moz is a huge player in the SEO space, a Seattle-based company that started off as a consultancy but moved into producing SEO software tools. Their website has its own blog but it previously hosted a community contribution blog called YouMoz, where anyone could contribute. If the post was of a high enough standard, it would be published, but if it really hit the grade, it would be promoted to the main blog, where it would receive a lot more attention and traffic as a result. I contributed to YouMoz five times over the years, and was delighted and proud to see two of my posts promoted to the main blog. The other site I mentioned – State of Digital – is a multi-contributor digital marketing blog, where I used to provide a post every six to eight weeks, although l contribute to it a lot less often these days.

Similar to blogging, I've received direct enquiries as a result of my guest posts – multiple from Moz and at least one that I know of from State of Digital. It all helps.

Create Resources that Benefit your Local Community

Another way to get onto the radar of prospective clients and networking partners is to create resources that might be of use to them.

I've managed to do this twice, both times on behalf of Computer Recruiter, my parents' IT recruitment agency. *(Note: just before publishing the book, they decide to retire, and – in doing so – closed the business. I just wanted to mention it just in case you look it up – or look these resources up – and struggle to find them.)*

In the first instance, when my parents' business turned 25 years old, I created "CR 25", a one-off-ish content marketing campaign where we published 25 blog posts in one month to mark and celebrate the business' silver anniversary. One of the 25 posts was a list and map of all the coworking spaces in South Wales. In addition to listing all the spaces available at the time (which I have since tried my best to keep as up-to-date as possible), I created a custom Google Map – using the Google My Maps platform (where you can create your own maps on Google Maps) – to mark and pinpoint all their respective locations. It was useful for people who wanted to give coworking a try and who wanted to see what was available in Cardiff, Swansea and other South Wales towns. As mentioned earlier, the Cardiff Start community has a strict no self-promotion policy, but what I've found is that I don't have to share it myself –

other people will do it instead. If someone starts a thread asking for coworking space recommendations, there's a good chance that someone will share my local resource – and it's exciting that this is continuing to happen organically, with no influence or physical effort required on my part. If you'd like to see the list and map for yourself, visit: seono.co.uk/coworking.

The second resource I created for Computer Recruiter was TechEvents.Wales. Launched in January 2018, it presented a list of upcoming tech events in the area on its homepage, having aggregated event data from sites such as Meetup.com and Eventbrite, automatically pulling in their data as-and-when new meetups are announced. This resource saved people from having to manually check, follow, or sign up to all the different meetups individually, and also gave a good at-a-glance insight into the busyness of the tech events scene in the local area – something that organisations such as Cardiff Start are keen to champion to the rest of the UK and beyond. On its blog, I also included a list of South Wales-based women speakers, because I was fed up with some events having male-dominated speaker line-ups and hearing the same excuses over and over again from the event organisers that they didn't know many women in tech. With over thirty-five women listed on it (as I write this), they have no excuse now. That particular post has also performed well, especially on social media.

Resources such as these are great for a number of reasons:

- Primarily, you can stick your name on them. Although they were projects created on behalf of my parents' business (technically a 'client'), there was still a Morgan Online Marketing link at the bottom of the sites, with "post by Steve Morgan" against all the blog posts.
- Secondly, I mentioned that people often shared the resources – and if it was shared on something like Facebook or Twitter, they'd often tag or mention me: *"check out this list of coworking spaces that Steve Morgan created."* In fact, despite Cardiff Start's strict no self-promotion policy, I sometimes managed to share them myself in a roundabout (albeit still natural) way: for example, if an event organiser created a post on the group announcing their upcoming event, I might reply saying *"oh, would you be happy for me to add your event to TechEvents.Wales?"* with a link to the site. More often than not, the response I received back from them was *"uhh, yes please!"* – who's gonna turn down some free promotion after all? It's a slightly cheeky way to share it in an altruistic

way, but without coming across as self-promotional.
- And speaking of which, thirdly, it's a gentle, non-pushy and somewhat selfless form of promotion. At the end of the day, these were marketing campaigns, with the aim of raising the profile (and SEO) of Computer Recruiter and their main company website. But if you can create content that will genuinely help people in the process, then even better.

Touch Base and Ask

The saying *"there's no harm is asking"* is cheesy as hell, but it's true.

If you have a gap in your capacity, don't be shy or afraid to ask people you know for help. Here's a few examples:

- **Touch base with old clients.** Depending on the reasons why they're no longer your client – whether it's the case that it was just a one-off project, or they didn't have the budget to continue working with you, or there was a change of direction, or some other reason – it's worth asking just in case their situation has changed and they need your help again.
- **Touch base with your main referral partners.** Do you tend to pass work to agencies

in semi-related industries, for example? There are a few web design companies I recommend, and likewise, if they know someone who needs SEO, they usually pass them on to me. It's always worth letting them know that you're currently on the lookout for new clients, just in case they know of anyone who might need assistance. In one instance, a contact said to me: *"oh I never pass people your way because I know you're always at full capacity!"* – so at one point when I *wasn't* at full capacity, I made sure he knew the change of circumstance.

- **Touch base with other referrers.** Beyond the more 'official' referral partners, who else refers you work? Friends? Family? Old colleagues? Go ahead and ask them too.

- **Touch base with people you've previously turned away (due to being too busy).** During hectic periods, when you're at full capacity, have you previously had to decline work? Now's the time to get back in touch with them. They might have moved on since then – by hiring someone else to do the work, or deciding that they no longer need the support – but then again they might be in the exact same situation that they were in previously (when they first contacted you), and therefore will still need your assistance.

- **Touch base with people you've previously turned away (due to a conflict of interest).** Have you previously turned anyone away as a result of a conflict of interest? In my case, I work on a one-client-per-profession basis, as I don't think it's ethical or moral for me to work with two businesses who are targeting the same keywords at the same time, as one is inevitably going to outperform (or 'outrank') the other. So if a web designer gets in touch for SEO advice and I'm already working with a business that does web design, then unfortunately I have to turn them away. At one point I had a Cardiff-based PR agency as a retainer client who also offered web design, graphic design, social media marketing, photography and video production as additional services, which meant that by working with them, I was 'locked out' of working with a lot of other potential clients in those industries. So when my retainer with them came to an end, I knew I had a list of web design companies, video production companies, etc. that I could get back in touch with and explain that I was able to work with them now (if they still wanted or needed my help).

- **Touch base with current clients.** Why not have a conversation about it with current clients? They're happy working with you and want to support you, so they may know someone who needs your help as well.
- **Touch base with other freelancers.** Have you passed work to other freelancers during times that you've been too busy to take on a new project enquiry? If the situation has changed and you now have availability, you could ask them to return the favour. It might be the case that roles

have reversed and that s/he is now too busy to take on new clients – so now they know that you have capacity, they can pass potential clients your way.

- **Put the word out on social media.** I've seen countless freelancers over the years post on Facebook, Twitter or LinkedIn saying that they have availability at that very moment in time. Don't be shy about doing the same. Ask your followers and connections for help. It's **not** a sign of weakness, if that's something you'd be worried about.

In Chapter 3, I suggested that you avoid approaching people that you don't already know. That point still stands here. Only contact people you have a past relationship and rapport with. Don't hassle strangers – not unless someone can make an introduction for you first.

If you've helped several other people in the past, you'll hopefully get your 'George Bailey moment' just when you truly need it. George Bailey is the main character from *It's a Wonderful Life*, the 1940s Jimmy Stewart movie that is my favourite Christmas movie (and one of my favourite movies of all time, full-stop). Potential spoiler alert warning: at the end of the movie, the altruistic and beloved-in-the-community George Bailey is helped by everyone he's previously helped during his most pressing time of need. If you have helped others in previous months and years but then find yourself in a quiet spot work-wise, hopefully others will spring into action and assist you with a referral or two when you need it. The more you've helped others, the more chance (and more likely it is) that others will help you in return.

CHAPTER 5
The Anti-Sell Formula

Ok, so Chapter 4 was a beast. For that reason, let's have a quick recap to pinpoint which parts tie in with the Anti-Sell ethos.

Why did I choose the term 'Anti-Sell' in the first place (other than the fact that it sounds so darn cool)? Because the goal of selling in this way is **not** to sell. At least not in a *Glengarry Glen Ross*-esque, schmoozy, heavy-on-the-biz-dev type way. Nope. Don't 'sell' yourself in the traditional way.

The first point is that you should 'put yourself in the shop window' (so to speak!) by showing off your expertise. Genuinely and legitimately set out to help people. Go to events and pass on your knowledge, and be available to help people with what they're struggling with. This is definitely one of the best ways to become recognised in your field, in my opinion.

Create stuff that helps people. You probably picked up on this after reading each of the 'Run a [Something]' subsections of the chapter. Run a meetup. Run a conference. Run a webinar. Run a podcast series. By running something, you put yourself at the forefront – which is great for personal branding. It's a nifty shortcut to being viewed as an authority in your industry, especially on a local level (say if it's a local meetup or conference). You might not be speaking at such an event, but you could still be hosting and presenting it – and at the very least, you organised the event and chose who you wanted to be involved and how it plays out.

Another point is that you'll hopefully get to a point where people spontaneously sell you *for* you. I discovered this when contributing to Facebook groups such as Cardiff Start. If someone leaves a post asking for a recommendation of an SEO professional, I might get name-dropped, which is ten times better than me name-dropping myself. We live in an age of recommendations and referrals, so inevitably *"hire this*

SEO professional called Steve" is so much better than
"I'm an SEO, hire me."

If you do all of that, you won't *need* to sell. You'll sell
yourself without even trying, and others will be happy
to sell you on your behalf. And that is a very, very
strong position to be in – an amazing position to be in if
you hate sales (like I do).

The remainder of this book will help you to get yourself
into this position, with tips and tactics all along the way,
including (in my opinion) the best way to get
testimonials, going niche, why size doesn't matter, and
much more.

You'll notice one thing though: with a lot of the tactics,
you have to put yourself out there. You have to make
yourself visible. I'm sorry, but you won't be able to
succeed in this way if you hide yourself away. You might
be thinking: *"that's easy for you to say, Steve, given
that you like to run events and go to events and
socialise and stuff!"* Yes, that's true about me, but I also
identify as being an extremely sensitive person who
struggles to handle negative feedback. I also have two
young children, and while I need to work the occasional
Saturday, I try and take off Wednesdays every week to
spend with the youngest, who's still a preschooler as I

write this. Despite these challenges or hurdles or whatever you want to call them, I manage to run a full-time business, write blog posts, run events and... err... write this book. Heh, maybe I'm just a glutton for punishment.

Whatever the case, this leads me onto the next chapter... but before we jump into that, I want to introduce you to the book's first Anti-Sell Story.

An Anti-Sell Story: Caryl Thomas

Caryl Thomas is the founder of the HR Dept Cardiff, a specialist HR support consultancy. HR Dept is a franchise, and despite being a UK-wide entity, Caryl runs the Cardiff area.

Caryl and I know each other through both being at Welsh ICE, my coworking space. Caryl has since moved to her own premises elsewhere (and has even begun to hire staff, which is brill), although she still visits and works from ICE from time to time, which is great as we have a catch-up whenever she does.

It's quite fitting that Caryl's story is the first featured in this book because it was the first one I received. We talked about the book while it was still being written, and she told me that the idea had resonated with her because of a keynote speech that she was asked to give to a group of university students, which led to an incredible opportunity to work with a big-name client in Wales. What's most impressive about the story is the way that the speaking gig came about, and also because the client approaching her afterwards was completely unexpected.

"My sister went on a yoga retreat and met a lady called Ita McNeil-Jones, who had started a recruitment company called Sitka," Caryl explains. *"My sister put me in touch with Ita via LinkedIn as we work in similar fields: HR and recruitment. We had a coffee up at Welsh ICE and kept in touch.*

"Sitka is a member of the USW Exchange (USW standing for the University of South Wales) and had been invited to sit on a panel discussing HR at the university's Newport campus. They were looking for a keynote speaker to talk to their students about careers in HR. I was put forward by Ita and went and delivered a speech. Also, on the panel alongside me

was one of the university's senior HR lecturers. Months later, Jo Duggan – the HR Manager of the Wales Millennium Centre in Cardiff – contacted me to help support her on a couple of projects, after the lecturer who had been with me on the panel recommended that she speak with me."

What's great about Caryl's story is that she really didn't expect anything to come from her keynote speaking endeavour – she did it simply because she's passionate about HR and wanted to help students who were interested in HR as a career choice. *"It just goes to show that I expected nothing from that speech as it was all about giving back to HR students – but I ended up with a fantastic new client,"* Caryl told me.

I've known people turn away opportunities that involve helping students, thinking that doing so will be a waste of time on the networking and personal branding fronts because students aren't necessarily potential clients or referral partners. But you never know who's going to be in that room with you... Take it from Caryl.

Find out more about Caryl and the HR Dept Cardiff at hrdept.co.uk/licensees/cardiff.

CHAPTER 6
But what if you're [x]?

Going through the list in Chapter 4, you might be thinking to yourself: *"yeah, easier said than done though, right?"* I appreciate that there's a lot to take in in that chapter – and like I said before, it's not intended that you try *everything* on the list (that would be outrageous, although a bit funny I admit)! You may find that some options sit well with you, or you might be thinking: *"well I've been considering doing [x,y, or z] for a while now anyway..."*

I appreciate however, that some options might be completely unfeasible depending on your personal situation. Without sounding cheesy, I'm really hoping that there's something for everyone in there. In this section, I offer my thoughts and advice on what might suit you best, depending on your current circumstances.

Feel free to leapfrog this chapter if none of these apply to you, but do take note of any that do. To summarise, we'll be covering, in order:

- What to do if you're already working in full-time employment,
- What to do if you have a family, especially young kids,
- What to do if you identify as being shy or an introvert,
- What to do if you consider yourself extremely sensitive, and
- What to do if you suffer from a chronic illness and/or you're an individual who has a disability.

What if You're Already Working in Full-time Employment?

This is the big one, insofar as it's probably affecting most people reading this book (at least those who haven't started freelancing yet, but want to).

If you've not yet set yourself up as freelancer, but your days are already filled by working a full-time job – and especially if it's a stressful, demanding job – then the idea of getting things ready on the side while still working your main job may not sound that doable or appealing. And you're right to think that.

However, you do **not** want to make the same mistake I made when I first started out. I didn't 'get things ready' in advance – I quit my agency job and planned to start everything freelance-y the following week. In my defence (sort of), I was working a stressful job at the time, and on my penultimate day working there I was co-running an all-day digital marketing workshop for local charities. So I didn't really have much time during the evenings and weekends leading up to my departure to prepare and plan ahead for my freelance business – I was either working late or absolutely knackered! Still, in hindsight, I should've really tried to make some preparations on the side, or I could have clung onto my 9 to 5 for a few weeks or months longer instead of quitting when I did.

My advice to you is this: however difficult or painful your current job might be, however much you're tempted to quit right now and join the wonderful world of freelancing, I urge you to consider making a start on doing some freelance work on the side – *alongside* your main job – and persevering until you have at least a couple of clients, or one big project ready-to-go. *Then* –

and only then – hand in your notice. Oh and make sure they're confirmed, signed-on-the-dotted-line projects, not verbal agreements or somebody saying *"yeah, sure, quit your job and then I'll hire you for some work after you've worked your notice period."* You can't count on that – and you don't want to be caught out *thinking* that you'll have work ready and waiting for you, only to discover that it's not the case when you finally start making the official transition to freelancing full-time.

I know what you're thinking: *"easy for you to say."* But genuinely, I made the mistake of transitioning into freelancing too early, without being properly prepared. Please don't follow my example on that front. Juggling both full-time work and freelancing won't be easy, but it won't be forever and hopefully the latter will excite you and spur you on into getting things sorted, so that you can fully take the plunge ASAP.

Also, make sure you have some money saved by. Cash in the bank will come in handy in the early days – trust me. You may have to pay for a few things upfront, such as a website, branding, business cards, computer equipment, software subscriptions, and so on – so you might find that the early days are heavy on expense but low on income. This should start to swing the other way once you've settled in and start to do lots of freelance work, with all those upfront, one-off costs now out the way.

Another semi-cheeky thing you can do is to start networking and going to mutually relevant events while still at your full-time job. Although you will be there to represent your current employer, it won't hurt to also use the event to network on your own behalf, but it's best to be reasonably subtle about it because there might be uncomfortable repercussions if your setting-up plans find their way back to your boss before you are actually ready to break your news.

What if you have a Family, especially young kids?

Do you know what I hate? Those so-called influencers on Twitter, LinkedIn or – god forbid – Instagram who post a list of what you have to do in your life each day in order to become successful. One of the main points will almost always be this: always get a full night's sleep. Every single night. Eight hours, no less.

...Yeah. Good luck with that if you have young kids!

I also heard an audiobook recently that said something like: *"you're never 'too busy' – just give up that TV show you watch or that video game you play in the evenings."* Like it's that simple. In that instance, I'd bet you good money that the author doesn't have any kids. Sure, this advice might be alright for people who don't have young children, but I have a four-year-old and an 18-month-old as I write this: I love them to bits, but holy hell are they horrendously poor sleepers! Neither of them can fall asleep at night unless mummy or I are sat with them, and they sleep in separate rooms, resulting in us sitting with them in their respective rooms until as late as 8pm on some nights. I don't know about you, but after sitting in a dark room for an hour or more, the last thing I'm in the mood for when I finally break free is to contribute to a webinar, write a blog post or respond to a Facebook group thread – I just want to chill, watch some TV and get an early night, especially after a full day of doing client work.

My wife and I are very lucky in that we have the boys' grandparents living nearby, so if I need to pop to an event one evening, the kids' nanny, bampy or mama can look after them. I know a few parents who don't have any grandparents or any support nearby and I genuinely wonder how they survive...!

I was also very fortunate in that I did a good chunk of my networking before we started a family. Our oldest son was born about a year into my freelancing career, but I'd been on the scene (so to speak) back as early as my Liberty and Box UK days, as well as during that first year of freelancing. So I guess you could say that I had a bit of a head-start on that front.

Even so, I still manage to squeeze in activities however, whenever and wherever I can. I usually do Cardiff SEO Meet planning during the evenings, as I'd rather spend my weekday daytimes concentrating on billable client work. Luckily, keeping a keen eye on Facebook groups and Twitter can be done on my iPhone, so I might do a bit of that while I'm sat with my youngest son, while he takes a million years (or so it always seems) to fall asleep each night.

Going to physical events is certainly trickier. Going to a BNI at 7am is near enough impossible these days, as I'm usually mostly responsible for getting the kids ready each morning, while my wife gets ready for work herself. Evening events and meetups are also often tricky to attend, for the aforementioned reason that the kids have difficult bedtimes. There are daytime events that you could explore, such as lunchtime networking events, so they could be an option. There are even some child-friendly networking events, such as BizMums, who run mid-morning events that you can take your kids along to.

And if going along to physical events simply isn't an option, then seek an alternative from my list in Chapter 4. What about online events? A lot of webinars take place during the day, especially those that are hosted in the United States during their office hours. If you're a stay-at-home mum or dad who cannot commit to events (online or offline), focus on tasks or activities that you can optimise around their naps. For example, contributing to a Facebook group can be done at any time really, so if your little one still has a nap during the day, maybe try and do it then.

I know it seems impossible to do all this extra stuff when you're juggling freelance work and parenting (trust me, I've been there – in fact I'm still there right now!), but I'm hoping that you'll be able to find a way.

What if you Identify as being Shy or an Introvert?

I appreciate that the word "introvert" can have negative connotations these days, and that it can be impolite to describe someone as such, so please understand that I mean no disrespect and do not mean to sound patronising when I use it in this context.

People often consider me an extrovert. I mean not in a 'weyhey, laddy-lad!' kinda way (I hope!), but it's true that I can go to a networking event and will happily chat to someone I didn't know until just then. But then again, that's kind of the point with events such as those: often, everyone is in the same boat, arriving and not knowing other people there, so it's kind of expected. And you're wasting your time (and money, if it's a paid event) if you go there and don't chat to anyone. I guess I've had years of practice as well – I doubt I was that 'brave' when I went to my first ever BNI, but by the time I went to my 10th one, I knew exactly what to expect, and even if it was my first time at a different chapter, I'd probably be ok chatting to strangers because I was familiar with the setup and format.

One tip for going to networking events if you consider

yourself deathly shy is to go to one where you already know at least one or two people present. You could even consider bringing a friend of yours along. The risk here is that you spend all your time clinging onto and chatting with the people you already know (and arguably they're the last people in the room you should be networking with, as... well... they already know you!) but it's certainly better than the alternative: not going at all.

It can be very helpful when some events publicise the attendee list before you go. So if you're deliberating whether or not to go based on who might be there, you can check the list for names that you know and recognise, which might put you more at ease. I know that this is the case for BNI (they list the names and companies of all the members of each chapter on their website) and some meetups (especially those run on Meetup.com). If the event has a hashtag, you can check to see if people have tweeted in advance saying: *"Looking forward to going to #EventName tonight!"* That could be another way to get an idea of who's going as well.

Similarly, with webinars, you might be able to watch one from the host's back catalogue before contributing to one yourself. This was my experience with Max Impact. I watched a few old ones, then watched one or two live, then I watched some live while leaving a comment or two on the corresponding Google+ page, then eventually 'sat in' on one. You don't have to do the last thing straight away: you can build up to it and slowly grow your confidence.

And if you're worried about having a disadvantage over any extroverts you know – especially if your local competitors seem like extroverts to you – then don't worry too much about it. In Daniel H. Pink's book *To Sell Is Human*, he talks about a number of studies, the findings of which indicate that there is absolutely no link between being an extrovert and being better at sales, so therefore there's no link between being worse at sales if you consider yourself an introvert. Just because someone is livelier and more outspoken than you are, it doesn't mean that they're automatically a better salesperson. So there's that as well.

What if you Consider Yourself to be Extremely Sensitive?

I fully appreciate that a lot of the tactics listed in Chapter 4 involve making yourself visible and putting yourself out there. It follows that doing so can lead to attention, and attention can lead to feedback and criticism – especially if you're going down the run-an-event/webinar/podcast/etc. route. Some (if not most) of the feedback and criticism you'll receive will likely be hugely positive, but you can't please everyone. Also, although possibly well-intentioned, some people may give unfair, nasty feedback that can be hurtful without that necessarily being their true intention.

I identify as being a highly sensitive person, a concept coined by Dr Elaine Aron. She's written a book about it called *The Highly Sensitive Person*, plus there's a few good offshoot books, such as *The Highly Sensitive Person's Survival Guide* by Dr Ted Zeff and *Making Work Work for the Highly Sensitive Person* by Dr Barrie Jaeger. Funnily enough, Dr Jaeger's book recommends self-employment as the ideal work choice if you identify as being an HSP – how funny is that?! Reading that was one of the main motivators for me to consider freelancing as a career choice. When I first discovered the concept of HSP, it was a big sigh of relief – I'd honestly thought that I was alone in feeling the way I did, but apparently as many as one in five people can identify with it.

When I run Cardiff SEO Meet, I openly welcome and encourage feedback from attendees – after all, it's the only way I'll discover if people find it worthwhile and where there might be areas for improvement. There have been one or two instances of some quite unfriendly feedback – ironically, from someone who loves coming to the events and I genuinely believe that he means well, but it's often worded badly and comes across a lot more harshly than I'm sure was ever intended. Even though it's that classic case of 'one in a hundred,' and I know from other feedback that the vast majority of people who attend are happy with each event, it still feels like a dagger in the heart when I read those words. I'll still obsess and worry about the one person who is unhappy, not the other ninety-nine out of a hundred who are. Nobody likes bad feedback, but I do wonder if other people can handle it a lot better than I can.

I don't know if there's a perfect solution for this to be

honest. I am a self-diagnosed HSP, but even so, I still network and run events and blog and so on, even though I know there's always a risk of receiving feedback from naysayers or even downright trolls. I guess I continue on because I realise that those instances are often extremely rare and miniscule in comparison to the positives, and that I'd rather carry on than not. In fact, I accept comments on my blog, and I think I've only received two or three genuinely nasty comments in total, in over seven years, across over 180 blog posts and over 800 published comments. But imagine thinking *"I'm never going to blog!"* because of just one or two potentially nasty comments out of hundreds and hundreds.

You'll often find that the biggest naysayers are those who *aren't* putting themselves out there. The guy who criticised Cardiff SEO Meet has – to my knowledge – never run his own events or meetups. So don't let people criticise and crush your efforts when they might not have done anything of the sort themselves. Keep on creating.

What if you Suffer from a Chronic Illness and/or you're an Individual who has a Disability?

I feel like I'm baring my soul and telling you all my secrets in this chapter...

In addition to identifying as an HSP, I've also spent the last six or seven years suffering from an on-again-off-again chronic illness. For the most part I'm fine, but if I have a flare-up then it can vary from being fairly mild – something that painkillers can usually keep at bay – to being near-enough debilitating. When the latter strikes, it can really screw up my workload, as it's not the best headspace to be in if you're trying to work on an important client project. It might also turn me into a bit of a flake, meaning that I'll cancel social plans at the very last second.

Freelancing has been perfect for me for when I do get flare-ups, as I can work on the days when I feel ok and just try and rest up on the more difficult days, even if it means swapping a weekday for a Saturday or Sunday. Despite being self-employed, I try to work as 'Monday to Friday / 9am to 5pm' as I can, but it's good to know that if I'm feeling rough on a Friday but fighting-fit on a

Sunday, I can make up the time on the latter day instead. I wouldn't necessarily have that luxury if I still worked a full-time office job.

If you suffer from a chronic illness, hopefully you'll be able to fit your activities around your better days. I try to work as hard as I can on the days where I know I'm ok – after all, you never know if the next day is going to be a 'bad day,' so if I put something off until then and then I get hit with a flare-up, it's not gonna be good.

If you have a chronic illness that makes leaving the house difficult, then consider the more 'online' activities from Chapter 4. You can still network with people in a webinar, or on a Facebook group, or on a Twitter chat. You don't have to be face-to-face necessarily. Do what works best for you and your particular circumstances.

A good and inspirational person to follow is Grace Quantock. Grace is a friend of mine who runs multiple businesses, one of which includes business coaching for people who suffer from chronic illnesses. She herself suffers from multiple chronic illnesses and is a wheelchair user. So if you identify as having either a life-long illness or a disability (or perhaps both), please don't think that the tactics in Chapter 4 may be too difficult to pursue. Grace is proof that you can perform very well in business, despite what life might have thrown at you.

The point I'm trying to make in this chapter and its subsections is that hopefully there are ways through for everyone in Chapter 4. Not only will you be thinking of focusing on activities that resonate well with you – and that play to your strengths and passions both as an individual and a business owner – but also those that work around the more complex issues that are also part of your life, whether that be juggling parenting, a full-time job or staving off a nasty illness (or perhaps all three). I don't want to patronise you and point out the obvious by saying that it might not be easy, but it's not impossible. And if you do fit any of these subsections (and especially the last one), you have my full respect and admiration. You can do this.

An Anti-Sell Story: Ahmed Khalifa

Ahmed Khalifa is an Edinburgh-based digital marketing expert who specialises in working with small businesses with WordPress websites. He's also one of the co-organisers (and in fact the lead organiser at the time of writing) of WordPress Edinburgh, and recently started to run Hear Me Out [CC], a blog that celebrates d/Deaf culture and shares inspiring stories from individuals within the community.

It was one of those classic 21st century meeting stories: Ahmed and I started following each other on Twitter a few years ago. We then first met in person at one of the brightonSEO events - if memory serves, in September 2014. A few years later, I was honoured to be invited on his podcast as a guest, in an episode all about building an SEO freelancing business.

For Ahmed, as a digital marketer with a specialised focus on helping WordPress sites, getting involved with WordPress Edinburgh – and therefore the local WordPress community – was an absolute no-brainer...

"As someone who is not only passionate about WordPress but also has a business that revolves around it, it made huge sense for me to be part of the WordPress community," Ahmed explains. *"This can be online and interacting with different people around the online world and offline by attending local events across the country and abroad.*

"But a huge part of that is also being part of the local WordPress meetup group, which in my case would be in Edinburgh where I live. My main purposes were to surround myself with like-minded people, be around those who are smarter than me, and – as part of the WordPress ethos – to give back to the community which has given me so much.

"What I didn't realise was how much being part of the WordPress Edinburgh group has played a huge part in the growth of my businesses. When you build natural relationships with other people, trust and honesty starts to form.

"And with that trust and honesty comes referral work too.

"The best thing about it is that it happened naturally, almost by itself. There were zero intentions from my side to go out and seek new clients, and I believe that being there, giving back and contributing back (and not expecting anything in return) can help with your business."

Ahmed also takes a lot of time to create useful content. I'll let him explain: *"Another aspect that helps to generate leads and enquiries is my content. I put huge emphasis on the quality and consistency of my content (perhaps too much in some cases). These are in written format, audio (podcast) and videos.*

"Content marketing is a huge topic and you can read countless books and articles about it. But aside from attracting traffic and leads, creating the right type of content strategically can help you to gain authority, respect and credibility within your field.

"And in turn, that can help your target market to trust you.

"Some of the feedback I have received because of my blog posts, podcasts and YouTube videos include: 'I contacted you because of your content', 'Your blog post has made it easier for me to work out whether you know your stuff or not' *and* 'I feel like I know you after watching your videos and listening to your podcast'.

"Even though collectively, my content has played a part in creating leads, I have had specific types of videos which have directly contributed to signing up new clients and creating bespoke training for them. Even more surprising is that these videos were not necessarily related to WordPress or digital marketing. They were actually personal. But this allowed me to

create a personal brand and to connect with the viewers, who in turn became my clients."

"What part of that has anything to do with using a sales technique?

"It's all because I went out there, put my face on the camera, put my voice online and wrote passionately about a topic that I knew would benefit my target market in some way or form.

"And with the intention of serving rather than expecting."

Find out more about Ahmed at iamahmedkhalifa.com.

CHAPTER 7
Getting out of your (Industry) Bubble

One of the takeaways you hopefully picked up on in Chapter 4 is that when it comes to attending networking events, meetups, webinars and so on, it's good to be semi-relevant, but not necessarily wholly relevant. What I mean here is that it's a good idea to hang out with people who *don't* do what you do, but who are still very much closely aligned to it.

If you're an SEO in a room full of SEOs, you're likely to be with competitors and peers, not necessarily referral partners or potential clients. However, if you're an SEO (and the *only* SEO) at a web developer meetup, or at a blogger conference, or as part of an online entrepreneurship community, or in a social media marketing webinar, then that can be a huge opportunity to be one (or perhaps the only) SEO contact for all the other people involved.

Don't just attend under the pretext of networking though. Make sure that you actually want to go and learn about what the event has to offer as well. When I went to a Cardiff-based conference called The Business of Web Design a few years back, its audience was almost entirely made up of self-employed web designers and web developers, because the theme of the conference was giving advice to agency owners and freelancers about how to run the business side of things. Now I'm not a web designer, but it was still an extraordinarily useful conference for me, as I too am affected by topics such as time-based pricing vs value-based pricing, educating clients, sales meetings and client relationship management. Take out the references to "web design," substitute "SEO" in its place, and there really isn't a huge amount of difference in what's being said. I still found it hugely beneficial – an added bonus to the networking side of things.

I won't linger on this point much more, as I appreciate that I covered it already – and passed on some other examples – during various parts of Chapter 4. But I've given it its own (albeit short) dedicated chapter because I really want to hammer this point home.

Let's quickly lay out a few more examples...

If you're considering going to meetups, and you're a freelance graphic designer for example, consider going to web design meetups, digital marketing meetups and so on. Web designers and digital marketers may have clients who need graphic design, but might not offer it themselves, so who are they going to give the work to?

If you're considering taking part in Twitter chats, and you're a freelance photographer, don't just take part in photography-related ones. Imagine what you can offer the #BlogHour blogger community if the topic one week is all about getting your blog's images looking right. And after you've impressed all the bloggers taking part with your photography knowhow, who are they going to think of the next time someone needs a photographer?

If you're a freelance copywriter, and you're considering taking part in webinars, don't just take part in webinars that are all about copywriting. What if you're the only copywriter taking part in social media marketing webinars or SEO webinars? Who are those attendees going to turn to when they need to outsource some copywriting work?

The possibilities are pretty much endless. And I don't know about you, but to me that's really exciting.

Obviously you'll want to track your efforts and over time try to figure out which of these activities has resulted in the most enquiries. Chapter 15 goes into more detail about charting your progress when it comes to your prospecting efforts. You may find that frequenting a weekly webinar isn't as effective as regularly attending a local meetup, in which case you can put less focus into the former and more into the latter going forward. However, as mentioned in earlier chapters, it's important to give multiple tactics a try – and to try them more than once – in order to see how they do for you.

CHAPTER 8
Go Niche

When I first became a freelancer, one of the most pivotal books I read at the time was *The Pumpkin Plan* by Mike Michalowicz. Mike is brilliant – not only does he give fantastic advice but he's got a great sense of humour too. I have the audiobook version which he self-narrates, and he sounds just like the character Saul Goodman from the TV shows *Breaking Bad* and *Better Call Saul*, which just adds to the amusement (at least for me, anyway)...

In *The Pumpkin Plan*, Mike compares growing a business to growing a massive pumpkin, in that those pumpkin farmers who grow freakishly large pumpkins to win pumpkin-growing competitions have to go through a very particular process. Anyway, if you've never heard of the book before, I appreciate that it might sound a bit silly (and weird), but if you take a look at his comparisons, you'll get what he means.

One of Mike's suggestions is to go as niche as possible. We've all heard the saying 'jack of all trades, master of none,' which is used when someone offers lots of very broad services but not necessarily a focused specialism. For example, I could be a marketer – offering help with all facets of marketing – but I decided to go niche into online marketing. I could be an online marketer – offering help with search engines, social media, email marketing, conversion rate optimisation and user experience – but I decided to go niche into SEO. In fact, when I first became a freelancer, I offered both SEO and PPC (the latter of which stands for Pay Per Click, the parts of search engines where you see the 'sponsored ads' links), but after a few years, I decided to drop PPC in favour of concentrating all my efforts on just SEO work. I could even consider breaking it down further and specialising within SEO itself. As mentioned in Chapter 4, there's an SEO I know who *only* does technical SEO audits, and he seems to do pretty well out of it.

Going niche isn't necessarily just a case of looking at

what services you offer – it can also be about who you offer them *to*. I do SEO for pretty much any business (or website, more accurately), but if I specialised in doing SEO for, say, only job and recruitment websites, then I have a potential edge over other SEOs when a prospective recruitment agency or job board client comes a-knockin', because I have direct, focused experience within that industry and topic area. I'd understand the usual SEO issues that plague job board websites, or the best websites to target for recruitment-related link building, and so on.

There are a number of benefits to being as niche-y as possible...

Firstly, you're a lot easier to refer. This is a trick I picked up in my BNI days, although I think this understanding is pretty much universal. Even if you are a full-service agency or freelancer, if you talk about specific topics then it's a lot easier to pick out and pinpoint what you do, rather than just unleashing a long list of services onto people. Also, if you specialise in something, it's so much easier to say: *"oh, he's the SEO guy"* or *"she's the web designer who specialises in WordPress websites within the weddings industry,"* or *"that company specialises in conversion rate optimisation in the travel sector,"* and so on.

Secondly, there's a certain stigma attached to 'jacks of all trades' – and rightly so, I'd argue. If someone juggles SEO, PPC, social media, email marketing *and* other online marketing disciplines, are they going to be as proficient as you would hope with the SEO stuff? How are they going to keep up with all the unrelenting, never-ending changes in the industry?

Thirdly, by going niche, you're seen as a specialist. You might end up being seen as the king or queen of a dedicated niche if you specialise in just one thing and become known for being good at just that one thing. This is a very strong position to be in if/when someone needs exactly what you offer.

In my opinion though, the best way to go is 'T-shaped.' I'm not sure who coined the term – I thought it was Rand Fishkin, who is a bit of a legend in the SEO industry and one of my favourite people in the universe, but even in his 2013 article on the subject, he references other sources, so he's probably not the originator. Anyway, being T-shaped refers to being a specialist in one area (the vertical part of the 'T') while having a bit of enough-to-get-by knowledge in other related areas (the horizontal bar of the 'T'). So for example, for me, I specialise in SEO, but I know a bit about PPC, social media marketing, content marketing and creating websites. My technical SEO friend would have technical SEO as his long part of the T, and all other areas of SEO – keyword research, Local SEO, link building, and so on – as the top part of the T. This is incredibly valuable as it shows that you understand the wider implications and impact of your specialism on other related areas. This is preferable to being an SEO who only cares about SEO to the point that they're stuck in their silo. It's better to be an SEO who focuses on link building topics that also improve social media marketing efforts, or who uncovers keyword research ideas that can drive a strong-performing content marketing campaign, for example.

In short: specialise, but at least have a working knowledge of other closely related areas. There are the sayings 'know a little about a lot' and 'know a lot about a little' – I guess this is the in-between. Know a lot about one thing, and relatively little (in comparison) about the rest.

An Anti-Sell Story:
Victoria Cao

Victoria Cao is the co-founder of Stray Pixel, a freelance graphic design studio that offers design, branding and illustration services. Prior to that, she worked at Gocompare.com – one of the big insurance comparison websites in the UK – in their digital marketing department as a content marketing executive and outreach specialist. We met at brightonSEO a few years ago through a mutual friend (Andrew Isidoro), who was one of Vic's colleagues at the time. We later bumped into each other a few times at Welsh ICE (my coworking space), when she first set up Stray Pixel.

The reason I've included Vic's story is because of the way she found her niche – and the advantage that that gave her. She's not just a graphic designer; she's a graphic designer with a background in digital marketing. This gave her an 'angle,' allowing her to offer a strong USP (unique selling point) against other graphic designers.

"I spent five years working in digital marketing before finally taking the plunge to go freelance, and I can say

without a doubt that the experience I gained during that time is what's allowed me to stand out in the industry," Vic explains. *"Having previously researched, designed, and promoted numerous campaigns during my time in content marketing, I'm fortunate to have a working understanding of how a variety of marketing channels work, and how best to design for them.*

"This has helped me to secure work with a number of digital and content marketing agencies since going freelance, and allowed me to pick up projects quickly without clients first needing to explain what it's for or how it'll be used. I'm able to consider the processes they go through behind the scenes (client sign-off, tone of voice, CMS), understand industry terms that other designers they've previously worked with haven't been familiar with, and sometimes even add value by suggesting what type of design might work best for their campaign.

"While I might not be a traditionally trained graphic designer, I love being able to work on these creative campaigns that I would otherwise have been pitching against many other similar people for. It's a niche that I definitely wouldn't have if I'd pursued this career

from the start."

Vic's process makes a lot of sense. Your average graphic designer may have trained in graphic design, but they may not fully understand what's required to make a piece of content that can be later used by someone in a content marketing executive-type role. But because Vic *has* been a content marketing executive in a past life, she knows what's required when creating content that not only looks good but performs well as well. She's sat on 'both sides,' if you will.

When I asked Vic to contribute her story, she pondered over the possible and the actual course of her freelance career: *"Sometimes I wonder how much further along I'd be in my graphic design career if I'd pursued this profession from the start. But then I stop and realise that it's really my experience in the last few years outside of the industry, that's really helped me to set up as a freelance designer,"* she said.

Vic also has some good advice for transitioning from a full-time job to freelancing, which I wanted to include because it complements my advice in earlier chapters: *"Bridging my income gap by taking a part-time job is the biggest tip I've given to anyone who's asked me how they too can start freelancing. It allowed me to rest a little easier knowing that at least my mortgage would be paid for at the end of each month, but most importantly it gave me the opportunity to try out being self-employed - I started freelancing with zero clients, never having done it before, so it was invaluable that I could first prove to myself what I felt I could do before committing to it full-time."*

Found out more about Vic and Stray Pixel at straypixel.co.uk.

CHAPTER 9
Finding the Good-fit Clients

In Chapter 8, I mentioned Mike Michalowicz's book, *The Pumpkin Plan*. Another great part of the book covers what he calls the Assessment Chart, where you list all your clients – past and present – and score them based on various criteria. You can tailor it to your needs and what's important to you criteria-wise.

I gave it a go myself a few years ago, scoring clients based on how much the project was worth, whether it was one-off or ongoing work, their potential for referrals or growth (i.e. extra work or upselling), and so on. I also included a few SEO-focused criteria, such as whether or not the client actually understood what the work was about (it always makes life easier when they do), and how collaborative they were in taking on-board my recommendations and getting them implemented on their website. Once you have all your criteria ready, you give each client a score of up to 3 in each column – with '3' meaning they're amazing in that area, '0' meaning room for improvement – and then add them all up to have a grand total at the end. *(If I remember correctly, Mike uses a grading system – e.g. A to F – but what I found is that if you use numbers instead then you can add them up to get an overall score for each client, making it easier to assess each of them in full.)*

That way you'll find out which are your best-fit clients. It's as simple as that. Not just your best and worst, but your best-fit and worst-fit – those that marry up with the criteria that are most important to you and the way that you like to run your freelancing business.

To find out more about the process, see it in action, and get a link to a template that you can use yourself, visit: seono.co.uk/chart.

It may sound like a bit of an obvious and boring exercise with predictable outcomes, but it was a real eye-opener for me, when I finally took the time to do it. I assumed it would be a waste of time, and that – surprise, surprise – my favourite clients would rank at the top. But I was wrong.

One of my so-so clients ranked at the top because I realised that they were flawless in all but one area, which was admittedly what was letting the side down. I think my actual favourite client ranked 2nd or 3rd. My least favourite client – a non-paying bully that ended up in a legal battle (but that's a *whole* other story!) – didn't even rank *last*! Nope, someone I knew from my school days had that honour. It's quite interesting to see how everyone lands and who your best-fit and worst-fit clients turn out to be.

The beauty of the Assessment Chart is that by helping you realise who ranks where, you can structure or restructure your business accordingly. What if all your favourite clients fit a specific type of service and/or industry? If you're a social media marketer and your Top 3 scoring clients were all Facebook Ads projects, maybe you should consider specialising in just offering Facebook Ads support from now on. If you're a copywriter and all your top scoring clients were financial services businesses, then maybe you've just found your new niche. Which ties in beautifully with Chapter 8.

As well as charting and comparing your clients past and

present, it's also important to chart your prospecting progress – but we'll come to that part of the puzzle in Chapter 15.

CHAPTER 10
The Solo Advantage: why Freelancers tend to beat (Larger) Agencies

When it comes to pitching to prospective clients and winning work, it can be super intimidating if you find out that you're up against an agency. After all, you're just one person; meanwhile an agency could comprise of anything from a small handful of people to dozens or even hundreds or individuals, most of whom also do what you do for a living too.

But you know what? Don't be intimidated. Be empowered. Freelancers are better than agencies for a number of reasons...

Firstly (and here's the obvious one): we're usually cheaper. Or maybe I should say that we're "a more cost-effective choice" rather than "cheaper," as the word "cheap" often has some major negative connotations associated with it. It's true though; as a freelancer, the main overhead is probably your coworking space or a small office, if you even have one (you might just work from home instead, eliminating that overhead entirely). For an agency, they might have to rent a large office premises, plus there'd be salaries and other overheads and costs on top. Freelancers are inevitably going to cost less.

Secondly, we're usually 'more experienced.' If you're a freelance social media marketer for example, you might have been doing social media – whether in-house or agency-side – for a number of years before taking the leap into self-employment. You know your craft. Whereas the agency might give the work to an inexperienced account manager or someone in a junior role. A client once told me about the time he'd hired an agency because of their experience and reputation, only to discover later that they had assigned to him an account manager who had only been in the job for just one week. Not just at the agency, mind you – in his *career*!

Who do you reckon the client wants doing the work for

them: the experienced freelancer, or the dude who was legitimately saying *"it's my first day"* just five business days ago?!

I appreciate that it's unfair of me to suggest that *every* agency ever would be guilty of this, but it's still something to think about. In that example, could the client be paying the higher agency fee but not receiving the expected quality of work because the work was passed on to a less experienced junior?

Thirdly, what you might consider to be a big client might be an agency's smallest client. Some agencies tend to go starry-eyed over the big companies; they want the big household names to be their clients, the ones who people recognise, the ones who'll earn them prestige, and especially the ones who'll help them to gain the big glitzy awards. That's not to say that they don't necessarily care about smaller businesses per se, but it might be less of a focus for them – such businesses would be their bread-and-butter after all, not their dream prize.

Lastly, and perhaps most importantly, the person doing the selling is usually the person doing the actual work – as in **you**, the freelancer! At an agency, there could be a huge disconnect between what the business development manager promises (or perhaps even *over-*promises) and what the account manager and his/her team can actually deliver for the client. Miscommunication can sometimes happen between both teams, from the sales process to the actual client service process, meaning that work might not be completed in the exact way the client had been expecting. Alternately, with the individual freelancer who initially 'sold' the work being the same person to complete it, there's less chance of a big disconnect between what's been proposed and what should be delivered. Again, it might seem like I'm being unfair and nit-picky, and I'm sure many agencies (especially the good ones) have this locked down.

But my main point here is that freelancers can realistically compete against agencies. We have our advantages, our pros, our strengths. If you're pitching for work and you're up against an agency, don't be disheartened. Don't think that you can only realistically compete if only other freelancers are pitching.

One of my clients is a large software and outsourced service provider for the UK financial services sector, with multiple offices around the UK and about a thousand employees. Before I started working with them, they'd previously used two agencies that were based locally to me as well as their HQ office. In both instances, they found that the agencies were fairly hands-off, to the point that the client didn't have a clear idea about what they were actually paying for and receiving each month. In the more recent instance (the second agency, the one which I was directly following and taking over from), all they got each month was a bog-standard report telling them how they were doing according to their Google Analytics data (something that they could've downloaded themselves if they wanted to), but absolutely little-to-no mention of what SEO work was actually being carried out for them. When I went on to take over the work, I was immediately more 'involved' than the previous agencies had been and therefore quickly won favour with the client. Over two years later, we're still working together on a rolling contract basis.

Ultimately it depends on what skills and solutions you can offer and the type of working arrangement the client prefers. For example, the client may prefer the perceived 'security' of working with an agency, or it might be the case that the agency offers more services than you do, or the workload would be too much for you to handle as an individual. This can hopefully all be worked out fairly early on – especially if it *isn't* a goer – so that it doesn't waste too much of your or their time.

Whatever the case, just remember that you can offer just as much – if not *more* – than an agency might be able to. Bigger doesn't necessarily mean better, and more people doesn't necessarily mean more or better work. There's a lot of value in being a freelancer. Be sure to remember this the next time you enter the sales process with a big prospective client.

An Anti-Sell Story: Marijana Kostelac

Marijana Kostelac is a freelance writer and content strategist, who works primarily with SaaS (Software as a Service) and marketing brands. Originally from Croatia, Marijana now lives in Dublin, Ireland.

I met Marijana at one of the brightonSEO conferences (September 2017, I think). At the time, she'd just made the leap into freelancing and self-employment. When I asked for her Anti-Sell Story contribution, she sent me back a detail-packed reply.

"My story is the one where I sort of stumbled upon the marketing world about 3 years ago (late 2015)," Marijana explains. *"Marketing piqued my interest when I was at a sales job, sat within earshot of the marketing team. Their conversations were more interesting than anything else, and I wanted in.*

"Guess what I did? I went through HubSpot's certifications, Google's online training, Moz's Whiteboard Friday videos and pretty much any free training I could get. I wanted to get a job in content or social media marketing, but although I now knew a lot, I had zero experience, so it wasn't working out as I had hoped. I also had zero connections and absolutely nobody in my network to introduce me to marketers at all. These were my key problems.

"This is when I reached out to Mark Scully (of Learn Inbound) to see if he needed help with his conference. I also asked him if he believed I needed to go to college to get into a marketing career, because nobody seemed to want to hire me. He replied with a confident 'no' and started to kindly introduce me to our speakers, attendees, and sponsors, which he still does to this day.

"Fast forward about 18 months to mid-2017, when I'm at the brink of leaving a job where I'm creating courses

*in marketing, but not practicing marketing. During
this entire time, my involvement with Learn Inbound
continued to increase, and Mark asked if I would go to
a conference aimed at bloggers and – as a Learn
Inbound representative – report from it on our blog to
bring some extra value to our audience. I said yes. A
few weeks later, thanks to the blog post I wrote about
a masterclass from that conference, I had my first
freelance writing client.*

*"The speaker that held the masterclass reached out to
me after seeing my blog post about him and asked me
to write for his company blog (he owns a video
storytelling agency). This ended up being a seven-
month-long working relationship and a five-figure
project. Another project I got directly from being with
Learn Inbound happened because an agency
approached me at our full-day event and asked about
my involvement with the event. When I explained it to
them, as well as my full-time job (freelance working
with SaaS businesses on content), they took my
information and within two weeks I was working with
them on a project with a Fortune 100 company.*

*"This entire series of connections led to me being a go-
to person because of a referral that wouldn't have*

happened if three or four people hadn't introduced me to each other. Connections are so powerful!

"On top of all this, podcasting got me on the content marketing and SaaS map. I interviewed other SaaS writers, agency owners, SaaS CEOs, content marketing consultants, and well-known speakers and personalities of the marketing world. What happened from here is that I became recognised as the 'content person.' This brought me a podcast interview on Dan Shure's podcast (who's a well-known SEO consultant), an online summit speaking gig (for which people send me kind messages about to this day) and real friendships with people I've only dreamed of knowing. They now support my projects, as well as send me referrals consistently (around 5/month – bear in mind that I only have the space for one or two new clients each month, sometimes not even that).

"This all happened because of the podcast. I wasn't a nobody anymore. I used to be terrified of speaking to anyone at events or on Twitter because I thought people would think I'm not experienced or known enough to do so. Now, I regularly spark and join conversations both online and offline, as well as intentionally reach out to people in the industry with what would be the most terrifying email even just over a year ago. It's usually something like: 'Hey, I really admire your work and have learned x and y from you over the past year! Let me know if I can support your work in any way.'

"This would have freaked me out before, but through friendships that have been created this way, I have received referrals for work with companies like AWeber and got on the radar of marketing leaders in companies like Scoop.it and Zapier, who I am so proud to say I've worked with.

"This is a whole lot of stuff, but I genuinely think that podcasting and Learn Inbound have turned me into this hyper-connected human being and it's what's genuinely made a difference. I have **never** said to any of these people that I need help finding work or getting referrals, but they did so for me anyway, and that's what true connections do."

Find out more about Marijana at marijanakay.com.

CHAPTER 11
LinkedIn can be your Friend: the Ultimate Testimonials Strategy

There's an emphasis on "can" in this chapter's title because I know some people who hate LinkedIn with a passion. If you identify with this crowd then hear me out before you skip this chapter, yeah? Who knows, you may even dust off your account and give it a go...

Some people's LinkedIn profiles are full of glowing testimonials where former clients or employers sing the praises of the person they have worked with. But how do you go about getting testimonials? One of the most traditional ways people ask for them is via email. The (happy) client emails back with his or her kind words, and you throw that text onto your website. This is fine n' all, but asking them to leave it on LinkedIn *first* instead is so much more powerful.

The fact of the matter is this: anyone can say whatever they want on their own website. Are the testimonials even genuine? Even if they all are, what's stopping someone from thinking that they're not? They could be genuine, but there's the possibility that they might be complete fiction. Sure, someone could go ahead and call the testimonial-giving company asking for a reference to double-check its credibility, but how often does that happen? Rarely, if ever, I'd wager. I even know one guy who used fake placeholder testimonials on his website before he launched it, but then either forgot about them or *decided to keep them* after it launched. I think they might still be on his website today...! Not good.

However, if your client leaves you a testimonial via LinkedIn (or a 'recommendation,' to use LinkedIn's own terminology) then you have a profile, a name and a face connected to it. It's hard to be 'fake' on LinkedIn, so inevitably a testimonial on that platform has a lot more authenticity behind it.

So that's my tip: get your recommendations on LinkedIn, *then* you can copy them to your website. The only exception of course will be any client who doesn't use LinkedIn – but that's a rarity these days. Most people are on it. I think out of the 25+ testimonials I've been given for Morgan Online Marketing over the years, only one of them wasn't left on LinkedIn for that exact reason.

In addition to this, when placing them on your website, consider including a link to your LinkedIn profile alongside some text that says something like: *"See these testimonials and more on LinkedIn."* That way, if someone discovers you through other means and sees your Testimonials page before checking your LinkedIn profile, they might go on to check out more of them on LinkedIn, which will hopefully confirm their initial thoughts about hiring you for work. And even if they see that link but *don't* delve onto LinkedIn to look at them, it's intended to be a gentle prompt to them to make them think: *"oh, s/he's got more testimonials on LinkedIn – got it."* I also do this on proposals: so a proposal may only include a small number of testimonials, taking up one whole A4 page, but there will also be a link to my LinkedIn profile suggesting that they can see more listed on there, should they wish to.

A quick side-note here: it might be worth asking permission of the recommendation-giver before you put their LinkedIn recommendation on your website.

Chances are, they'll probably say yes (I'd be surprised if they didn't), but I mention this because some LinkedIn profiles – and therefore recommendations – have strong privacy settings to preclude them from being seen by the public, whereas on your website they'd be fully public. I think doing this check might be considered a bit over-the-top, but then again, in this day and age of GDPR, the old saying *"asking for forgiveness is easier than asking for permission"* doesn't really hold as much water as it used to.

Aside from LinkedIn, I suggest doing – or at least watching out for – the following as well:

If you have your own blog or freelance site, have a Testimonials page on it. It's a no-brainer.

And don't just put testimonials on your Testimonials page and nowhere else. Put some (your best) on your homepage. Put a couple on service-specific pages – in fact, you could even consider matching testimonials up to their services. For example, if I were to get a testimonial for doing some keyword research work, I could put that particular testimonial on my dedicated Keyword Research landing page. An added bonus here is that the review will likely be contextually relevant to the page's content (as it's likely to mention the phrase "keyword research" once or twice in its text), therefore potentially helping with that page's SEO in the process.

I'm going off-course a bit now, but while I'm on the subject of reviews... If you have a listing on Google Maps for your business – known as a Google My Business listing – then watch out for randomly-left reviews. In fact, it might be worth safeguarding your listing by asking some of your happy clients to leave you a review on Google as well as on LinkedIn. If there's a satisfied-enough client who wants to support you, then they may be happy to go to the effort of copying and pasting their LinkedIn recommendation over onto Google as a Google review as well. Years ago, Google only showed the average rating for a business if there were at least five reviews, but now, all you need is one. You don't want your only review to be a random 1-star review, therefore meaning that you have an average of exactly 1 out of 5 stars... To make matters worse, a more recent phenomenon (as I write this) is the Google Local Guides programme, which essentially replaced Google Map Maker. People who contribute to Google Maps – whether it's correcting the location of a footpath, answering questions about a business's opening times, or leaving a review for a business – are awarded points, which can be used for things like discounts on Google Play, which is Google's app store. It's gamification, pure and simple. What it means though is that people can leave random reviews on businesses in order to get those points, and Google has no way of knowing if the person was actually a customer or client of yours or not, which can make them difficult – even impossible – to remove. So in addition to my aforementioned LinkedIn strategy, it might be worth getting a handful of Google reviews as well. Better to be proactive than reactive.

Anyway... Testimonials aren't the only way to make yourself look good, y'know...

CHAPTER 12
Awards: the Only thing you'll need a Marketing Budget for

If you follow some of the tactics listed in Chapter 4, then hopefully you won't need to do much more marketing or networking beyond that.

There is, however, one form of marketing investment you may want to consider: award submissions.

For the most part, my marketing budget has been minimal. All I've ever really spent money on is a website, branding and business cards (and I'm still using the original run of 500 that I had printed five years ago, although they've nearly all run out now – finally!). Cardiff SEO Meet sort of counts as marketing for Morgan Online Marketing, but even the expenses generated by that are (mostly) covered by sponsorship money. Other than that, I don't think I've spent a penny: no paid search ads on Google or Bing; no paid social ads on Facebook, Twitter or LinkedIn; no promotional materials; no event exhibitions; not even event sponsorship. Nothing.

...Except for award submissions.

It's ironic that I mention this as a tactic – purely because I've never actually won an award. Although in my defence, I've not entered a huge number of awards over the years either, but depending on the award in question, even being a finalist is big deal.

In recent years I have submitted a few client campaigns that I felt performed extraordinarily well, as well as my blog in a few different blogger awards. As a result, my blog was a finalist in the Wales Blog Awards once, the UK Blog Awards thrice, and CR 25 – the campaign that I mentioned in Chapter 4 where I published 25 blog posts in one month in line with my parents' 25th business anniversary – was a finalist in two categories in the UK Search Awards 2015. That last one was a pretty big deal to me because the majority of entrants and finalists in the awards are usually big SEO agencies and in-house teams. To give you an idea, the winners in 2017 included Verve Search, BlueGlass, Expedia and

GoCompare. I appreciate that you've probably not heard of the first two, especially if you don't work in SEO, but take my word for it that they're two impressive and well-respected SEO agencies. So in 2015, amongst these industry behemoths, there was little ol' me, touting his parents' wares, feeling completely out-of-place and 'not worthy' *Wayne's World*-style. In fact, I believe that I was the only freelancer who was a finalist that year.

The big value in being nominated for an award is what you do with that news. When I found out that I was a UK Search Awards finalist, I blogged and tweeted about it. My coworking space also featured it on their blog and I added it to my LinkedIn profile under the 'Honours and Awards' section – I just made sure to emphasise that I was shortlisted and not a winner. I also added a mention of it to my email footer, which was huge when talking to prospective clients, or even my current clients. In fact, one of my current clients saw it and replied saying: *"You've been nominated for two awards? Wow!"* It can act as a reassurance to clients and prospects that you are actually pretty good at what you do.

The downside to all this positive promo is that awards

can run expensive. Some awards are free to enter, while others (usually the good ones) require an entry fee. Fees I've paid have ranged from £40 to £200 – that's per submission *and* per award organisation. Yowza! So, if you have one campaign that you're entering into multiple categories and with several different award organisations, it can all add up. And what if you don't land a single nomination? It can be a massive, seemingly fruitless drain on time and money. Not only that, but if you *do* become a finalist, there are extra costs involved; after all, you don't want to *not* go and find out that you've won. There's the cost of the awards ceremony ticket (which can cost as much as the submission fee – if not more), plus transport and accommodation. When I went to the UK Search Awards 2015's ceremony in London, I spent over £500 – maybe even close to a grand – in order to enter and be there on the night.

Not only that, but it's not unheard of for some awards organisations to be really corrupt. A guy I know used to run one and he openly admitted to me that despite who the judges chose, he ended up having the final say on who got shortlisted, and often leant towards finalists who he thought would book the most tickets for the event, ultimately earning him the most money. I could picture him sat there thinking: *"hmm, should I let the solo freelancer become a finalist, or the agency with a dozen staff who might go on to book a whole table?"* To this day I don't know if he was either kidding or if he's just a unique example and an extreme case, but if other awards organisations do something similar then it is inevitably unfairly weighted against freelancers and small businesses who enter awards. Even if he *was* kidding, I feel sure that certain fringe organisations do it anyway.

Despite the last few paragraphs, don't let me put you off. Being able to say that you're an award winner or a finalist is a big deal. I'd love to be able to add the phrase "award-winning" to my blog and freelance site one day: "award-winning freelance SEO consultant" has a much nicer ring to it than just "freelance SEO consultant," don't you think? "Multi-award-winning freelance SEO consultant" sounds even better, if a bit over-the-top. And while it may not win you clients directly (unlike other forms of marketing), being shortlisted and winning awards raises your credibility immensely. So you may want to consider it as your main (and perhaps only) form of self-marketing going forward.

An Anti-Sell Story: Prabhat Shah

Prabhat Shah is the owner of Online Seller UK, a digital marketing and ecommerce consultancy and training provider, with a particular focus on businesses who sell products through eBay and Amazon.

I met Prabhat because he asked me to speak at Online Seller Wales – one of the meetups he used to run in Cardiff – back in 2014. A year or so later, when Kelvin Newman – organiser of brightonSEO – asked if he knew anyone who could recommend an Amazon SEO expert as a potential speaker for his conference, I proposed Prabhat. What started out as a speaking gig at the conference has since turned into a fruitful opportunity for Prabhat, as he hosts a dedicated Amazon SEO training session at each twice-yearly brightonSEO conference.

"I get regular referrals just being a trainer there." Prabhat explains. *"More recently, I also decided to exhibit there. Not many freelancers exhibit at brightonSEO, so I consider myself really fortunate to be able to do so.*

"One of my speaking gigs at brightonSEO led to another great enquiry just recently, when one of my talks was recorded and turned into a podcast. The prospective client heard the podcast recording, and based on that, they hired me for three months' consulting work doing Amazon SEO work for their business."

As an added bonus, Prabhat has also found that speaking at the conference and running training sessions there makes the 'sell' much easier.

"Beyond the above, I've gotten a lot of other enquiries thanks to brightonSEO as well. I find that converting them is a lot easier and quicker compared to other enquiries I might get, because being involved with the conference – in the way that I am – is a big trust signal."

Find out more about Prabhat at onlineselleruk.com.

CHAPTER 13
Keeping your Composure: How Total Embarrassment led to a Dream Client

From feel-good chapters about testimonials and awards, to... complete humiliation.

Quite fitting that this is Chapter 13...

I want to tell you a story about how keeping my cool in a situation where I wanted to rage led to working with a wonderful new client.

Admittedly, a lot of the tactics found in Chapter 4 mean that you have to put yourself out there. And being bold enough to put your head above the parapet can attract criticism or even trolling. I discovered this first-hand at one of my early speaking gigs.

It was a design meetup in Cardiff. My talk gave SEO advice aimed specifically at web designers, such as how to optimise images for SEO, ways to get around having a text-light website (as Googlebot relies on text to understand the purpose of a webpage), and so on. It was already pretty intimidating speaking to a design crowd, as some web designers and developers still have an uninformed view of the SEO industry, thanks to its spammy reputation back in the day. I felt as though I gave a good talk, which was followed by my friend Warren Fauvel, who gave an incredible talk about how the design industry was under threat by do-it-yourself tools such as Canva, which could cause some designers in the future to lose out on work. To this day I still consider it to be one of the best talks I've ever seen, and it was pretty obvious that he blew my talk out of the water. I'm just glad that I went on first and not second...!

As the speakers, Warren and I each had to choose a book ahead of time, something that we thought would be useful to the audience, which would be given away at the end of the event as raffle prizes. I chose *The Art of SEO*, an SEO textbook that covered a lot of the fundamentals of SEO, particularly the stuff that is always true and rarely changes. I thought that I would be given the opportunity to explain why I chose the book and explain that it's a textbook that you'd grab for reference as-and-when you need it, not necessarily a read-in-one-sitting-from-cover-to-cover type book. Sadly, I wasn't given that opportunity...

Instead, the event's sponsor introduced the book. He *had* read it all in one sitting (apparently something of a tradition of his that he used to do as part of the giveaway, which I didn't realise until the night itself) and complained that it was a boring book and felt sorry for whoever would go on to win it. Lovely! Thanks buddy. My book was drawn first, and lo and behold, when raffle numbers were called out, nobody claimed it: either the people with the winning tickets had already left the meetup, or they didn't want to lose their chance to win Warren's book (given that they only had one raffle ticket each), so kept schtum. It got to the fourth attempt before someone finally – and somewhat reluctantly – accepted it, who later told me that they didn't really want it. Even one of the event co-organisers – the one responsible for running the event's social media – sarcastically took the mick out of me and the book via the event's Twitter profile. Charming.

I was absolutely gutted. I had given up my time for free to speak at the event. It's not just 30 minutes you're sacrificing when you do a talk; it took hours beforehand to plan the talk, prepare the slides and run through it a few times. A lot of effort goes into it.

After I do a speaking gig, I tend to write a blog post explaining how it went and including anything that's useful, such as a SlideShare deck embed, a video embed (if it was filmed), photo embeds, tweet embeds, and so on. In this instance, I was also going to talk about how angry I was at that sponsor for talking badly about my book choice, but I bit my tongue. Looking back at the post now (which is still live on my blog), the only reference I made to it was by jokingly saying: *"Just don't ask me how the book giveaway went!"* Hah!

Ultimately, keeping quiet ended up being a good move on my part.

A year or two later, a web design company approached me saying that they were redesigning a website for a client and wanted me to take care of the SEO requirements. The end-client was someone I'd wanted to work with for years, and even one of the agencies I'd previously worked for had desperately wanted to work with them, so it was a pretty big deal to me. I ended up winning the work and I now work with the end-client directly on an ongoing retainer basis.

I asked the web design company how they found out about me. Unbelievably, it was through that event. They'd been in attendance; they'd seen my talk and were impressed with my SEO knowledge. I couldn't get over it. I asked them what they thought about the whole book giveaway debacle and they told me that while they thought I was harshly treated, it didn't affect their view of me. It just goes to show that sometimes we worry about things far more than we should do or need to.

I still think back to that talk and how I might've handled things differently in its aftermath. If I had reacted angrily about my treatment, would I have still gotten the enquiry that followed? Perhaps. They might not have seen the post-event fallout – whether on my blog or on Twitter or wherever it might've taken place – but what if they *had* done? What if they thought to themselves: *"actually, let's look for another SEO professional for this project..."*? I would have lost out on what went on to be an incredible opportunity.

It's so important to keep your professional cool in circumstances like the one I've described above. Recently, there has been some major debates and fallouts on a Facebook group I'm a part of, which has included discussions on improving the take-up of women speakers at local meetups and events, and a few (in my opinion) 'threatened' men have given their views indicating that doing so would result in fewer opportunities for men, like some silly reverse-sexism thing. One individual in particular (who I won't name) was extremely vocal about it, and then went on to say that despite regularly contributing to the group, he never received any enquiries from people within the community. I believe at least one person in the community pointed out that his behaviour *might be why* that was the case...

How you conduct yourself in person and online – especially if and when you feel like a wronged party (whether or not you are is an entirely different matter, of course) – is so important if you want people to pass you work.

So remember these three pivotal words: **keep your cool**. You'll appreciate that you did.

CHAPTER 14
How to handle Freebie Favour Requests

There's a very sensitive subject in the world of freelancing, which I like to call the two f-words: "freebie" and "favour".

I'm sure there are myriad blog posts out there that cover this subject in more detail – about if, when, how and why you should do work for free, or whether you should never ever do so – but I'd like to include my thoughts on the topic and my experiences with it.

In my line of work, as well as clients paying for me to collect data, do research, design strategies and implement tweaks for them, a lot of people just want advice. Does x apply to them? What's the situation with y? What's this news about Google doing z nowadays?

So, as you can imagine, I get a fair few requests whereby someone sends me an email or a tweet, or walks up to my desk at my coworking space and simply asks: *"Have you got a minute? I have a quick question..."* And more often than not, the answer will almost always take much longer than a minute...

There's a bit of a running joke in the SEO industry that you can answer any SEO-related question with *"it depends,"* as usually you have to find out more info or dig deeper into the issue – and when that happens, the 'quick question' suddenly becomes a lot more time-consuming. Of course, a lot of people don't realise the complexity involved, so I can't hold it against them *too* much.

The difficulty with freebie favours is the best way to handle them. If you jump straight in with a *"well my hourly rate is £x, you can pay me to help you"* type attitude, then you risk looking very Scrooge-esque, but at the same time, people have to understand that you're running a business.

These days, my approach is to help someone maybe once or twice, but at the same time encourage them to think about whether they can benefit by taking it further themselves. For example, their query might be a quick question about how to add keywords to a webpage, so I might make the point that they might not be the *right* keywords, so is a quick bit of keyword research in order? This might not be in-budget for them to consider right now, but at least it gets them thinking about valuing other people's work and – in my case – taking SEO more seriously. I could even say something like: *"here's a quick tool to dig out keyword ideas for yourself,"* and if they struggle with it, or want to make sure it gets done expertly, there are plenty of SEO businesses out there, including mine.

I understand that this issue might be different for freelancers in different industries. For example, if you're a graphic designer and the request is for a free logo, then it immediately gets more awkward because a) that's not a five-minute job, and b) they're jumping straight into something that's a paid service. Asking for a bit of free advice is one thing, but asking for a service to be carried out for free is taking advantage. So you may want to handle the advice in this chapter completely differently to the way that I'd potentially handle such a situation – and that's fair enough.

There's only been one instance where I had to ask someone to stop asking for free advice. At that point he'd probably contacted me four or five times in a relatively short period of time, always dangling the *"I **will** hire you one day"* carrot, but the final straw came when he asked me something that he could have quite easily figured out for himself. I said that I wouldn't be able to help him for free any more, and that from now on he could hire me, and that my hourly rate starts at £x. Funnily enough I never heard from him again after that. Just be careful of people who will leech, leech and leech. So make sure that you don't let yourself get sucked into this type of behaviour from people.

Interestingly, while writing this book, I had an instance where I felt that somebody had taken advantage of me, but it worked out well in the end. An old friend contacted me saying that he'd buy me a coffee or lunch if he could pick my brains for SEO advice for his new business venture. I said yes because his previous startup had failed, so I had sympathy for his past situation and imagined that he may need help for his second attempt, assuming that he might be launching another cash-poor startup. When I met with him, I found out that he now works in a high value sector and that he has a business partner who's happy to *"throw money at anything"* – his words. I was a little irritated by this, truth be told. You're telling me that you can probably actually afford my time but only wanted it for free (or for the cost of a coffee/lunch)? I kept my cool (hey, remember Chapter 13?) and continued to give a bit of my time for free, but I thought to myself that if he came back wanting more free help in the future then I'd immediately start the conversation about paid work – heck, they could seemingly afford it, after all. It turned out that a few days later, he wanted to come back for paid work – *he* suggested it, not me. So in a way, offering a bit of my time initially for free (which, to be fair, you would do when you meet someone for the first time about a project, during the sales process) led to him wanting to work with me on a more official paid basis. Score.

So, sometimes, giving a bit away for free – even if you don't necessarily want to – can be a good way to get someone interested in working with you on a more professional, actually-pay-invoices basis. Just watch out for them leeches though...

An Anti-Sell Story: Annie Browne

Annie Browne is a VA (a virtual assistant) trading as Hello My PA. She helps clients with CRM, business admin, social and email marketing, blogging, data entry, business admin and also offers a whole bunch of other services.

Annie and I met each other at Welsh ICE, the coworking space where we're both based. In fact, we're based in the same coworking area (as ICE has a number of coworking areas dotted around its campus), so I regularly catch up with Annie on the days when we're both in at the same time.

Like me and many other freelancers first starting out, 'selling' was the biggest challenge Annie faced in her early days in business:

"The concept of selling was the biggest hurdle I had to face when becoming self-employed," Annie explains. *"I heard so many times from various people that if I wanted to be in business, I would always have to 'sell'. Turns out that it wasn't selling that was the problem, it was the connotations attached to that word.*

Convincing my potential clients that they should use my services because I say all of the right things, isn't a good foundation for a working relationship."

In addition to freelancing, Annie enjoys co-running the Freelance Heroes Facebook group, which currently boasts over 5,000 members. *(You might remember me talking about it briefly back in Chapter 2, where I cited some of its polls data.)* Annie's goal was never to take advantage of her position as one of the group's admins; she only wanted to help and give back to the freelance community – and co-running a Facebook group for freelancers to share advice and to help each other out was her way of doing that. At the end of the day, you could say it was purely a side-project or hobby, so she never expected or intended for it to give her networking and marketing a boost as well.

"For me, demonstrating my abilities and positioning myself as a 'go to' person is key in forming the 'know, like and trust' factor. That is why running communities like Freelance Heroes – or being an active member of communities such as coworking spaces – works so well for obtaining new clients. It allows a wider audience to see you in action and enables you to build relationships where 'the sell' isn't

the aim."

The great thing about Annie's story is that she didn't get involved with Freelance Heroes or join Welsh ICE to network – she did them because she likes community-running and coworking, respectively. The networking and sales side of things only became apparent *after* she'd been involved in both avenues for a while. Like a happy added bonus to the whole thing.

And that's the beauty of Anti-Selling: do social activities that you love and you'll end up getting known through them as a result. You won't *have* to sell.

Find out more about Annie and Hello My PA at hellomypa.co.uk.

CHAPTER 15
The Brinley Method: Charting your Progress

Despite me writing this book and telling you my non-sales-y sales techniques, as you'll know by now, I struggled with sales in the early days of my freelancing career. As mentioned in an earlier chapter, it took a good six months or so until I was at full capacity for the first time. Those first few months were make-or-break.

Fortunately, around that time, my coworking space had just started to offer mentorship opportunities to its members. I was paired with a business management consultant called Brinley Groves, who's an expert in sales. We sat down a few times and he gave me some really useful advice on the sales front (some of which has made it into this book), and months later I suddenly had more work on my plate than I could handle, so I no longer needed to meet with him on a regular basis – consider it a *"my work here is done,"* walking-off-into-the-sunset moment.

One of his tips, which has stuck with me, is to chart your progress. It seems obvious to do this with current clients – i.e. keeping a record of what you worked on and when, how long it took you, etc. – but Brinley meant on the sales/prospecting front. In other words, keep a spreadsheet* of every enquiry you get and make a note of everything you can think of related to it: the business name, the industry, the type of work, the size of the project, whether it's one-off or retainer, the value, how they found you, and – perhaps most importantly – whether or not it converted into actual work (and the reason for that if it didn't). Was it because you were too busy to take on the work, or something else? Maybe they considered you too expensive. Or maybe the communication suddenly stopped and you were left in limbo. *(I hate it when that happens, don't you?)*

* Well, I say "spreadsheet"... I've never invested in CRM (customer relationship management) software, but you could use that instead I guess. Although that might be a bit overkill for a solo freelancer – I think CRM systems

are intended more for multi-department companies, such as agencies, but I might be wrong.

The idea is that over time, you can analyse the results and get a clearer idea of what's working and what isn't. What percentage converted altogether, or by industry? Is there a pattern between all those that didn't convert? Is there any form of seasonality, where you noticed an influx of enquiries during a certain time or month of the year? Tying into your marketing and networking efforts, where and how did they find you? Taking this further, where and how did the *ones that converted* find you? It's all well and good thinking *"that speaking gig resulted in a lot of enquiries"* but if not even a single one converted then was it really that strong a marketing tactic after all...?

I call it 'the Brinley method' in honour of its creator. Once you start, make a mental note to always update it as-and-when you're dealing with new enquiries. You don't have to include all your past enquiries if you don't want to, e.g. if you consider it too big an undertaking to look back and go through them all. Just start today and do it from now onwards. You'll still get a good number of prospects and enquiries to analyse afterwards.

CHAPTER 16
Generosity: Passing work to Others when you're Too Busy

Reciprocity is a strong factor in business relationships. If you help someone, they'll feel compelled to help you in return.

The main ethos behind BNI – the franchise of worldwide business breakfast networking groups I've mentioned a few times in previous chapters – is "Giver's Gain." If you give people business, they will want to give you business in return. Obviously it's meant and intended in a cross-industry way, so if I give a social media marketing referral to a freelance social media marketer, he or she may give me an SEO referral in return. But the same can apply within your industry, i.e. in my case, giving SEO work to another SEO professional.

Why on earth would you want to give a lead to another freelancer, I bet you're thinking?! Well, if you're an agency (and in Chapter 17 I'll briefly touch upon transitioning from freelancer to agency), you can just keep growing and growing – and hog them all for yourself, mwahaha... *ahem*. In other words, you can just keep adding employees to be able to accommodate the increasing workload. But if you're a freelancer, you might only have a finite number of hours per calendar month to commit to work, so if you've hit your ceiling and you get an enquiry, then you may have to turn it down or give it to someone else.

Remember all the way back in Chapter 3 when I said there were outbound sales and inbound sales? Well, if you're doing outbound sales and you're at full capacity, then... stop. Turn off all your Pay Per Click ads. Stop cold-calling (if you're doing that). But if you do some of the things I mentioned in Chapter 4 – which lean more towards inbound sales – then enquiries aren't just suddenly going to stop. They'll keep coming in. You've hopefully gotten a good reputation by now, and people will continue to enquire about working with you, regardless of whether you can accommodate them or not. Additionally, you might not just stop going to meetups or running your webinar or cancel your upcoming speaking gigs, just because you're full-up with work – there's a good chance that you'll continue with those commitments.

I remember having a good one-to-two-year period where my capacity was full-up with ongoing retainer work, with no flexibility to do any one-off work on top. All my clients were happy working with me on an ongoing basis and none of them wanted to end their retainers. This meant that I didn't need to do sales or write proposals or any of that malarkey for over a year. It was bliss. I still continued to get enquiries though, and without even trying. That's not intended as a humblebrag by the way – it's just the way it was (and is).

When I'm in this situation and I receive a new enquiry, I either outright turn it away or pass it on to someone I know and trust to do a good job in my place. One of the people I tend to pass these leads onto started off as a freelance SEO consultant like me, but has since gone on to grow his business into an SEO agency. As I write this, he's 'graduated' from being solo to having about five employees in an office, which is amazing. Have I inadvertently created a local competitor? Perhaps. But he's also been a long-term sponsor and supporter of Cardiff SEO Meet. He's even tried to return the favour once or twice, when a prospective client hasn't seemed the right fit for him but might be more suited to me. It's "Giver's Gain" in action, folks... My old BNI buddies would be proud I'm sure.

This works even better if you turn away work that's a poor fit for you – based on the progress-charting you've done with the *Pumpkin Plan* Assessment Chart (Chapter 9) and what I called the Brinley method (Chapter 15) – but could be a good fit for someone else instead. For example, I tend to turn away ecommerce SEO enquiries... Ecommerce websites (i.e. websites that sell products online) tend to have a very specific set of SEO challenges, but I've only ever worked on a handful of ecommerce websites in my entire career and have very little experience with today's ecommerce platforms (such as Shopify), so I tend to pass them on to people who specialise in doing SEO just for those type of sites. In return, if and when those specialists get an SEO enquiry for a B2B service provider's website, they'll probably (hopefully) consider passing it on to me.

The only other thing I'll say on this front is this: I feel

awful even saying it, but be careful with your use of the word "recommend." I once heard a horror story of a graphic designer friend of mine who recommended a web designer to a client, the project went pear-shaped, and the client decided to try and sue both the web designer *and* the graphic designer, the latter included in the wrath because he was the original referrer of the former. I don't think the disgruntled client got very far in their quest, and situations like this are one in a thousand I'm sure, but even so, you don't want stress like that in your life. There's also the notion that if you refer Person A onto Person B and Person B ends up being unhappy with the work provided by Person A, then it could reflect poorly on you – even if it doesn't get as far as the courtroom. So, with that in mind, I usually use phrases like: *"try Jo Bloggs, it's her specialism"* rather than *"I recommend Jo Bloggs"* – just in case. It's essentially the same thing being said, just phrased differently. It sounds awful even having to think that way, and it sort of sounds as though you're not really actually recommending them (even if you do wholeheartedly recommend them), but it's better to be safe than sorry.

Anyway, there's another thing you can do when you hit

full capacity but enquiries keep coming in: maintain a waiting list. Remember in Chapter 4 when I said that you can get back in touch with people you'd previously turned away? This is what I tend to do. As I write this, I have about a dozen businesses on my waiting list. Now there's a good chance that when I do have capacity and subsequently contact them to ask if there's still work needing to be done, they'll have moved on by then, and that's fair enough. But what if their situation is the same? What if they didn't hire anyone for SEO after all? Or what if they hired someone, it didn't work out and they're looking for help once again? You never know unless you ask them.

Being too busy has an impressive aura around it as well. When I turn someone away because I'm at full capacity, I sometimes get responses such as: *"glad to hear that business is going well"* and *"wow, you must be good."* People like to want what they can't have; this might mean that when you *do* have capacity and you approach them at a later date, they'll be even more inclined and excited to want to work with you than they did previously – making the sales process even easier.

An Anti-Sell Story: Dan Spain

Dan Spain is a freelance graphic designer who also runs Rabble Studio, a coworking space in Cardiff Bay aimed at freelancers, particularly those in creative industries. As I write this, its members include copywriters, journalists, designers, illustrators, artists, and developers. I've worked there for the occasional day or two in the past and I think it's an awesome place in a great location. I've known Dan for years, and our mutual love of the *Final Fantasy* video game series is something we usually end up talking about when we do get the chance to see each other in person (I think the discussion revolved around *Final Fantasy IX* the last time I saw him)...

A quick note here: in Chapter 4, I advised *against* running a coworking space. Sure, go ahead and join one, but running your own space can become a massive drain on your time, which could negatively impact your freelancing efforts as a result. That said, I wanted to include Dan's story – despite it conflicting with my earlier point – because he set up Rabble with the intention of *wanting* to run a coworking space alongside his freelancing duties, which is very different.

"Building communities and enabling your own network can present opportunities and collaborations," Dan explains. *"If you do not have a network or a community, make steps to create one. If you put people in the same place, amazing things can happen. Creative people naturally want to work together, and members of Rabble have worked together on bigger opportunities because there is a varied skill set in the room. Animators work with designers, designers work with copywriters, and so on. Individual freelancers have teamed up to tender for big companies and have won on the basis that they are a collaborative team and **not** an agency with higher overheads."*

Dan told me that running a coworking space has positively impacted on his freelancing business as well, as it has led to more referrals and clients – and an even better *calibre* of clients.

"Yes, I'm a designer, but running a coworking space took my work and clients to the next level, as I had a legitimate business and group of people backing up my professional services. Over time I have placed more focus on running the space of course, but this is a

result of my work and interests changing naturally. Running the space has also enabled me to take on work that I want to do, instead of feeling like I have to take on anything and everything just to pay the bills. So it's really been a win-win."

I love a good success story. If your freelance business is your core focus then my previous point will still stand, but I thank Dan for challenging it and for being a healthy and positive exception to the rule. And of course, when Dan talks about *"building communities,"* it doesn't necessarily have to be a coworking space: it could be an online community, a meetup or something else entirely. The option is yours.

Find out more about Dan and Rabble Studio at danspain.co.uk and rabble.studio, respectively.

CHAPTER 17
Growing from a Solo Freelancer to a Fully-fledged Agency

As mentioned in earlier chapters, I used to take part in a weekly webinar called Max Impact. Run by Seattle-based SEO consultant Max Minzer, it covered a different SEO topic each week, with each show featuring a guest speaker or two. On top of that, people like me and other SEO consultants and agency owners would hop in and share anecdotes, case studies, war stories and more. I was honoured to be the guest speaker one time, on the topic of – quite fittingly I guess – networking tips for SEOs.

Each show ran for an hour and they were recorded using Google+ Hangouts On Air, which saved them onto YouTube afterwards. Once Max hit the 'stop recording' button, participants would often stick around for a chat. Sometimes people would chat briefly, then sign out after a minute or two, but sometimes we'd stick around and chat for longer. In some instances, you'd get more insightful chatter in the unaired few minutes following the show than what might've actually been covered on the show that week. That's not a dig at those particular shows' content by the way, but the fact that someone might have shared something really useful that they had been reluctant to share earlier.

Like me, Max is a freelance SEO consultant. After one of the shows, he said to the rest of us: *"guys, I need to ask your opinion on something."* He went on to explain that he'd hit full capacity client-wise, and that he was considering growing his solo consultancy into an agency. We all congratulated him, excited to hear the news. However, he went on to explain that he didn't really want to grow into an agency, because he was happy working on his own, and that he didn't want the hassle of hiring and managing employees. But he said that it felt like a moral obligation to hire staff, because it would be his way of contributing and 'giving back' to the local economy. By *not* hiring staff, therefore, he felt he was being selfish and un-entrepreneurial. I could see his point, but told him that it was **entirely his choice** whether or not he wanted to hire employees.

I've started this chapter with this story for this sole reason: it is **entirely your choice** if you want to grow into an agency. You may not want to, and the good news is this: you don't have to. We may see other freelancers, startups or small businesses grow from a one-person sole trader or a two-person partnership, to ten or a hundred employees or more, which is the traditional and obvious way of 'growing' in business, but there are other ways to grow. You can grow your business in a purely financial sense, by gradually increasing your hourly rate and day rate as you become more experienced and take on bigger clients. That's still 'growing' your business – without hiring additional bodies.

I'm not best equipped to give you detailed advice on how to transition from working solo to manning the helm of a multi-person agency. Apart from being the first employee in a new agency that went on to hire dozens of staff, I have zero experience in running or growing an agency.

My point for including this chapter is to talk about how the points in this book can aid you well – if and when you grow your business into an agency.

Discovering Potential Employees

I started running Cardiff SEO Meet for a number of reasons. Firstly, the obvious one: no one else was running a regular SEO event in Cardiff. I also had a background in events management before becoming an SEO (I used to run live music events at university and loved it – switch the guitar and drums for a laptop and a PowerPoint presentation and it was pretty much the exact same premise). It was also a good way to get my name out there and to meet potential clients.

There was also a less obvious reason: it was a good way to get to know potential *employees* for my business. I had no interest in turning Morgan Online Marketing into an agency when I first started out, but there was no harm in getting to know people working in SEO in South Wales, just in case that situation ever changed in the future. Funnily enough, after a few events had come and gone, one of the regular attendees emailed me their CV on the off-chance I was hiring.

If you go to events, meetups, conferences or whatever,

you get to know who's out there. If you run an event, it's an excellent way to meet future employees and get to know them. After all, if you attend an event, you may only chat to a handful of people each time. But if you *run* the show, you can get well acquainted with the vast majority of attendees, especially if they're regulars.

So, as well as networking for future clients, make a mental note of anyone you meet who could be potential employee material.

Empowering your Employees

If you get to the point where you're hiring employees, you might want to involve them more closely with what you're doing. If you tend to go to a lot of networking events and meetups, bring them with you. It's a good way for all sides to bond, get to know each other and build mutual trust, by showing that you trust them enough to promote your agency alongside you. Plus, they could help you out on the networking front: for example, while you're chatting to people, they may be chatting to *different* people, expounding advice and wisdom in your agency's name. You'll cover more ground this way. Better yet, once they're confident enough, they could even go to *different events entirely*, covering even *more* ground. Whew!

If you're running events, why not ask if they want to get involved with running them? Heck, if they're a regular attendee (see above) who has since become your employee, they may jump at the chance if offered. Added bonus: it takes the pressure off you, especially if you tend to run them singlehandedly, as I do with Cardiff SEO Meet.

As mentioned above, while I've had no experience in hiring and managing employees (except for a bit of unofficial managing and training during my time at Liberty), I'd wager that a more involved and trusted team member would grow in confidence, which would result in better retention and better performance.

Don't force it on them though, obviously. Not everyone will want to help you to run your event, podcast, webinar or your <fill-in-the-blank>, but give them the option at the very least.

They might even suggest doing something that you're not doing already. For example, I run Cardiff SEO Meet, but I've never touched podcasts. What if an employee I were to hire is completely podcast-obsessed, has always wanted to run one, and now wants to run one in my agency's name? I'd say two words to them: hell yes!

Taking Altruism Further

Encouraging employees to get involved in your Anti-Sell style efforts can take the altruism aspect further. Picture the scene: as a solo freelancer, you might be already contributing advice – and/or running events that contribute advice – which reflects well on you as an individual. Now you're running a team of people and *they're* contributing advice to people. Not only will you be altruistic in your community because your agency is helping others, but also because your employees are operating under the same ethic.

I know a lot of what I've said in this chapter – heck, maybe even this book – might seem obvious. But *that's the whole point*. This stuff isn't exactly rocket science. But equally, it isn't exactly something that everyone is doing – or wants to do, either. If no one else local in your industry is thinking about their business in this way and doing this type of stuff, but you are, then, well... you're going to stand out. Big time.

An Anti-Sell Story: Francesca Irving

Francesca Irving is the founder and managing director of Lunax Digital, a full-service marketing agency with a focus on the health, beauty, fitness and leisure industries.

Like a number of the other Anti-Sell Story contributors, I met Fran through my coworking space: she was based in the same room as me when she first moved in and then later moved into her own office unit with a fellow Welsh ICE member, Alexis Hughes, whose company – Mila & Pheebs – offers subscription boxes containing stationery and activities for children. Moving into her own office made sense for Fran as she had plans to hire employees and grow Lunax into an agency.

Out of the eight Anti-Sell Story contributors in this book, I've included Fran's story last because it ties in well with the previous chapter about growing into an agency.

Despite Fran's success, she didn't have an easy start –

especially when it came to sales...

"My first ever job was in recruitment - which was basically sales," Fran explains. *"And I was rubbish at it. So when I started my business, the thing that terrified me the most was the dreaded selling part. Was I supposed to cold call businesses from the phone book? Or knock on doors? As I had a little bit of work to start me off, I didn't think about it too much but instead, focused on improving my presentation and public speaking skills.*

*"I signed myself up to run workshops and give talks at events, booking myself in for as many as possible over the year. After the first workshop I ran, I had a small queue of people waiting to talk to me afterwards. Was I selling my services without realising it? After each workshop, talk, or event, I **always** had a queue of people wanting to find out more about what I did, or ask questions that they perhaps didn't want to ask in front of the audience.*

"It didn't take long for me to realise that maybe this could be my sales strategy. I started to write my talks and workshops to not only educate the audience on the topic, but to also show my knowledge and authority on the subject. For example, I'd drop in examples of my

work, my qualifications, or how I had tackled similar problems that they might face. I wasn't directly selling my services, but I was subtly telling the audience that I 'knew my stuff'."

Before even knowing her backstory, I had asked Fran to speak at my meetup (Cardiff SEO Meet), as I like to have a mix of talks at the events, including those that cover subjects that aren't necessarily SEO-focused, but are still closely related and therefore still of interest to attendees. So for example, Fran gave a talk at one event about using cognitive biases on websites and its effect on conversion rate optimisation.

"One particular talk that I gave – at Cardiff SEO Meet – led to quite a bit of work. Speaking at an SEO event as a digital marketer, but not offering SEO as a service (at the time) was weird – but beneficial in the end. Most people in the room knew about SEO, but didn't know quite as much about my areas of expertise in digital marketing. I networked with a lot of the attendees afterwards and ended up landing a weekly digital marketing consultancy job, a website UX design project, and later on I linked up with another SEO agency to advise on UX for their clients, as well as making many other contacts. I definitely would not

have got that work any other way.

"I then took this technique and tweaked it slightly to add to my sales strategy. I joined lots of Facebook groups for freelancers or small businesses and networked a lot online. I even launched a podcast with my friend Alexis about balancing business life with babies. I'd use these platforms to offer advice and answer questions on marketing. I would even offer to do very small jobs for people free of charge, as they would usually take me literally two minutes. Once the relationship and reputation was there, it was easy to help out and land paid jobs."

There's a lot to unpack in Fran's story. Speaking at events, contributing to online communities and running a podcast have all helped her and her business on the sales and networking fronts. Even giving people a little bit of free advice – a sometimes sensitive subject that I covered back in Chapter 14 – has been a good way to start a relationship with potential clients and to get the ball rolling into possible paid work further on down the line.

Fran's business is a prime example of the Anti-Selling method in action. You don't have to 'sell' in order to sell your services.

And on that note, I'll leave you with the last line of Fran's contribution... *"After about a year in business, I'd gone from absolutely hating sales to loving sales. It doesn't have to be cold calling."*

Find out more about Fran and Lunax Digital at lunaxdigital.co.uk.

Closing Thoughts

I've never really enjoyed or have been excited about sales. Some people love the thrill of the sell – but it's not for me. I *do* love working from coworking spaces, attending meetups and running a meetup though. I love meeting people and getting to know them. I love making new friends, such as fellow freelancers who are in the same boat as me. I love helping people and giving them advice. And that activity has resulted in making lead generation a lot easier for my business.

Are there times when I can't be bothered? Absolutely. Are there times when I want to stop doing Cardiff SEO Meet, because I'm fed up with venue, catering or logistical issues, or the attendee who made nasty comments online after one of the events? Hell yes. Are there times when I just want to play video games or watch TV instead of writing a blog post or commenting on an entrepreneurship group on Facebook? Yes, yes, there definitely are! And are there times when I don't want to waste money on an award submission that might not amount to anything? Yep. *(That last point actually happened while writing this book by the way – that's £180 I ain't getting back...!)*

But nothing's ever easy, or smooth, or painless. I love doing all those things, despite the times when they're occasionally a headache, stressful or seem utterly pointless – but I'd much rather do them than the alternative: absolutely nothing. Doing nothing is the equivalent of hiding in a cave, both social-wise and business-wise. For the most part, doing all the stuff I've been talking about is fun and it ties in to my passions and my strengths – and if that results in an enquiry or two or five in the process, then happy days. In fact, the last client I started working with discovered me by coming to Cardiff SEO Meet; the one before that was a fellow member at my coworking space; the one before *that* was a referral from a speaking gig I'd done; and so on. None of them came through ads or cold-calling or anything like that. Everything was achieved due to my Anti-Selling efforts – doing stuff that I enjoy doing.

And that's ultimately the point: tie in attracting clients with what you love doing. Reread Chapter 4 and pick out the tactics and ideas that resonate with you. Heck, come up with *new* ideas that I might not have thought of, but that essentially follow the pattern laid out in Chapter 4.

We've all heard that cheesy saying about how if you do what you love, it won't feel like work. Substitute the word "work" with "sales" and that's the case here. Do something (or things) you love, get yourself out there, and let the leads and enquiries come to you.

Happy Anti-Selling, folks.

ANTI-SELL

Further Reading

Throughout this book I've mentioned numerous books and resources that can help you on your Anti-Selling journey. Here's a list, with a bit more info about each of them, plus a few more for good measure.

A quick note: None of these authors paid me a fee to be included, nor do I get a commission if you buy any of them. I recommend these books 100% wholeheartedly – because I actually really like them.

ReWork
by Jason Fried & David Heinemeier Hansson

ReWork is probably my favourite business self-help

book of all time, and a big influence on *Anti-Sell*. Why? Because *ReWork* is also quite rebellious in nature: it goes against the grain of traditional business advice but makes excellent recommendations in spite of that. It was recommended to me by a client (thank you Scott of TestLodge!) and on the first listen (I bought the audiobook), I fell in love with it. While listening to it in the car, I used to scream *"YES!!!"* after sentences I agreed with – which happened a lot. And probably sounded weird if I had my car window open. But there we go.

Some of its takeaways include:

- Other people's failures are other people's failures, not yours. So when people talk about the survival rate of freelancers, small businesses and startups, just remember: if other people fail, that doesn't mean you will too.
- Plans should be called "guesses." I remember freaking out when I had to put together a business 'plan' for some funding that I was seeking in the early days of freelancing (if I remember correctly, it was funding to cover my first year's membership at my coworking space). How do I know how my business is going to do next year or the year after that? And that's precisely the point. Call them guesses. To quote the book: *"Start referring to your business plans*

as business guesses, your financial plans as financial guesses, and your strategic plans as strategic guesses. Now you can stop worrying about them as much."

- Everything you do is marketing. This ties in very closely to the message of the book you are currently reading. Marketing isn't defined by adverts and promotional materials – it's literally everything you do. Every. Single. Thing. You. Do. Every email you send is marketing. Every invoice you send is marketing. Just because you've won a client, it doesn't mean that the marketing stops there for them. Every action you take can leave an impression on someone – good or bad.

I could go on and on, but I'll stop there. If *Anti-Sell* has resonated with you, and you haven't yet read *ReWork*, pick up a copy. I'm sure it will resonate with you as well.

While writing this book, Fried and DHH released a new book: *It Doesn't Have to Be Crazy at Work*, which – as you can probably guess from its title – addresses the sensitive subject of work-life balance. It's worth checking out as well.

The Pumpkin Plan
by Mike Michalowicz

The Pumpkin Plan is a special book to me. Whether you're just starting out, or you've been running a small business for a while and you've hit a rut, there are some great tips in it. As mentioned in earlier chapters, it has advice on:

- How to go niche when it comes to targeting clients.
- Creating your own Assessment Chart, which can be used to score clients on certain criteria, in order to help you to detect which clients are the best-fit for you.
- Tactics for cutting bad-fit clients in a way that won't cause any animosity, fallout or professional embarrassment.

Mike also has another good book called *Profit First*, where he recommends paying yourself first before paying bills, whereas typically we do the opposite (we pay our bills and then keep what's left over as profit, however big or small that amount may be), so it's worth checking out what he has to say on that as well.

To Sell Is Human
by Daniel H. Pink

"We're all in sales now."

In Chapter 2, I touched upon the phenomenon of the 'typical' salesperson, citing the movie *Glengarry Glen Ross* as a classic example. *To Sell Is Human* further investigates this somewhat old-fashioned stereotype, suggesting that salespeople of this nature are near-enough a thing of the past. If anything, we're *all* in sales – especially these days. While we still have 'obvious' types of sales, such as the process of asking a client to give you money in order to provide a service in return, we might also conduct certain tasks or habits that may not seem like sales but totally fall under that category. In a broader sense, sales is the process of asking someone to part with their time, money or resource somehow, in order to get something back that benefits you. So in other words, sales is essentially the process of moving or persuading someone to take action. When Daniel conducted a survey asking people if they work in sales, he found that while one in nine people considered themselves a salesperson in the traditional sense, when it came to 'non-sales selling' or moving/persuading others, the ratio was much higher.

If Chapters 2 and 3 piqued your interest especially, and you're interested in learning more about how sales has 'shifted' in its meaning and behaviour in the last few decades, then *To Sell Is Human* is worth taking a look at. A lot of what Daniel covers is backed up by psychological studies, and the book even includes selling tactics such as mimicry, the best style of positive self-talk, and in which order you should appear if you're part of a series of agency pitches and you want the best chance to succeed. It's an interesting read.

Start With Why
by Simon Sinek

"People don't buy what you do, they buy why you do it."

Simon Sinek's TED talk covering this topic is the third most popular TED talk of all time, having been viewed more than 40 *million* times on the TED website. He explains that most people in business talk about what they do, before saying how they do it, then lastly say why they do what they do. He then goes on to argue that the most inspirational people and businesses – think Apple, Martin Luther King Jr. and the Wright Brothers – start with *why* they do what they do, and *then* talk about the how and the what, i.e. the reverse of the usual order. Effectively communicating the "why" part of your core marketing message can make a huge difference on how you are perceived by others.

Youtility
by Jay Baer

"Smart marketing is about help, not hype" – this is the core message of *Youtility*.

The book starts off with Baer using a real-life example of a swimming pool installation business coming close to going under as a result of the 2008 economic downturn. In an attempt to drum-up more business, the owner started writing blog posts that answered frequently asked questions and also covered issues and problems that his customers often had to deal with. He literally sat down and wrote blog content covering every single possible question someone might ask him. Over time, his website became a go-to source for all help on swimming pool purchasing decisions, with some arguing that its popularity has made it the world's favourite go-to source on the subject. His efforts led to more customers for the business, and he also found that it led to better educated, easier-to-sell-to and therefore easier-to-convert customers.

The rest of the book explains how you can utilise Youtility – in the same way as the swimming pool business – and why it's the best way to market yourself now and in the future.

The Highly Sensitive Person
by Dr Elaine Aron
and
Making Work Work for the Highly Sensitive Person
by Dr Barrie Jaeger

I only necessarily recommend these books to people who resonated with the relevant subsection of Chapter 6. When I first discovered that I was an HSP, it was life-changing – not only because I felt like a freak growing up and thought that I was the only person who felt this way (these books revealed that this is far from the reality), but because Dr Jaeger's book has a chapter in it that recommends self-employment as viable career option for HSPs. And now I can confirm that he was right.

***

When compiling this list, I realised something really sucky: it's a very white male list, with only one woman author included. So if you can recommend any sales or freelancing books written by women and/or minorities then please do let me know, as I would love to read them. You can contact me at: seono.co.uk/contact.

.

Acknowledgements

A lot of people helped me to write this book.

Firstly, I'd like to thank everyone who shared with me their stories:

- Ahmed Khalifa
- Annie Browne of Hello My PA
- Caryl Thomas of the HR Dept Cardiff
- Dan Spain of Rabble Studio
- Francesca Irving of Lunax Digital
- Marijana Kostelac
- Prabhat Shah of Online Seller UK
- Victoria Cao of Stray Pixel

I'd also like to thank Peter Carless of Xanthe Studios as part of the above list, who also provided an Anti-Sell Story.

The following fellow Welsh ICE members kindly gave their time, thoughts and feedback on an early chapter-by-chapter rundown and synopsis of the book. A big thank you to them as well:

- Alex Kavel of GTalent
- Caryl Thomas of the HR Dept Cardiff (again!)
- Finola Wilson of Impact Wales
- Gareth I. Jones of Town Square
- Greg Bednarski
- Russell O'Sullivan of Digital Thrive
- Teifion Jordan

I'd like to thank Ben Potter, a business development mentor to digital agencies and freelancers – your course on sales at brightonSEO in 2017 was fantastic. I'd also like to thank Brinley Groves – of 'the Brinley method' fame covered in Chapter 15 – for meeting me a few times during my early freelancing days in order to offer me his help and wisdom at no cost. And I can't *not* thank the wonderful George Savva, who was my business mentor for a number of years during the middle years of my freelancing career.

A massive thank you to Welsh ICE, my second family. Y'know I used to hate it when the word "family" was used in a business sense, but quite honestly, you *are* my second family. I freakin' love you guys. Gareth I. Jones obviously gets a mention for being the main founder (alongside Mandy Weston, Anthony Record MBE and

Will Record), but it's the current ICE team who deserve a ton of credit: Jamie McGowan, Huw Williams, Rachel Jane Harris, Llinos Neale, Pauline Brame and Lesley Williams. Diolch yn fawr iawn.

Thank you to Jane Oriel for proofreading and editing this book. Thank you to Emily Hicks of Studio Hicks for providing the fantastic cover illustration. And thank you to Marina, Steve and Christian of Bengo Media for working with me to record the audiobook version of this book. *(Fun fact: years earlier, in a different life, Marina was also the wedding planner for my wife and I! It's funny how these things turn out, huh?)* Thanks also to Jonathan Robinson for letting me pick his brains about the self-publishing process, and Darran Hughes for providing PDF eBook formatting advice.

An enormous thank you goes to Bernard and Marilyn Morgan, a.k.a. my parents, Mum & Dad ("M&D" for short), "the folks," Nanny & Bampy, Maz & Bernie and probably many other nicknames and aliases besides. You've been massively supportive of me over the years. You are my biggest inspiration.

Thank you to my loving (and very patient) wife, Emma. And also to my two boys. Y'all make me very happy to be alive.

And last and probably least (to twist the famous saying!), the person who told me that I'd *"never last a day in self-employment,"* as mentioned way back in Chapter 1. Thank you. No really, I mean it: thank you. You encouraged me more than you ever could have known. Ironic, huh? Your casual, throw-away criticism instead helped me on my path, rather than hindering it. How do you like them apples?

Oh and thank **you** (yes, you!) for reading this book. I hope you found it useful. Tell your friends, etc.!

Thanks for reading!

About the author

Steve Morgan is a freelance SEO consultant based in Cardiff, South Wales, UK. Trading as Morgan Online Marketing, he has worked with a variety of businesses offering SEO consultancy services since May 2013. He also runs a blog called SEOno and a meetup called Cardiff SEO Meet. He has a wife, two children and two cats (sadly, while writing this book, this line originally said "three cats," but one of them died before the book was finished – R.I.P. Gilby).

More personally, Steve is a big rock music fan (his favourite bands include The Wildhearts, The National and Rocket From The Crypt, for anyone who cares) and also likes working out, swimming, red wine, RPG video games, Pokémon GO (yep, *still* playing it!) and playing Dungeons & Dragons with his friends up at Welsh ICE.

He dislikes writing about himself in the third person, making this paragraph pretty much unbearable to write. It's a good thing it's the end of the book though, right?

Follow Steve on Twitter: @steviephil

https://morganonlinemarketing.co.uk/

https://seono.co.uk/

Printed in Great Britain
by Amazon